WISDOM
IS NOT
ENOUGH

REFLECTIONS ON LEADERSHIP & TEAMS

ISBN 13: 978-1-59298-373-5

Library of Congress Catalog Number: 2010943015
Printed in the United States of America
First Printing: 2011
14   13   12   11   10   5   4   3   2   1

Cover and interior designs by Emsster Design Company

BEAVER'S POND
PRESS

Beaver's Pond Press, Inc.
7104 Ohms Lane, Suite 101
Edina, MN 55439-2129
(952) 829-8818
www.BeaversPondPress.com

To order, visit www.BeaversPondBooks.com or call 800-901-3480.
Reseller discounts available.

VOLUMES NOT FOR INDIVIDUAL SALE.

WISDOM
IS NOT
ENOUGH

REFLECTIONS ON LEADERSHIP & TEAMS

JEFF APPELQUIST

Award-Winning Author of
Sacred Ground: Leadership Lessons
From Gettysburg and the Little Bighorn

To my three best girls,
Faith, Anna & Lucia,
who are the light of my life

*"To accomplish great things,
we must not only act,
but also dream; not only plan,
but also believe."*

– Anatole France

CONTENTS

Introduction 1

PART ONE:
DECISION MAKING

CHAPTER ONE: *Go With Your Gut — But Not Always* 8

CHAPTER TWO: *Assess Risk Properly* 12

CHAPTER THREE: *Collaborate Effectively in Decision Making*. 17

CHAPTER FOUR: *Use the Right Data* 21

CHAPTER FIVE: *Be Aware of Cognitive Roadblocks to Good Decision Making*. 25

CHAPTER SIX: *Small Decisions Matter* 29

CHAPTER SEVEN: *Develop a Decision-Making Process*. 33

CHAPTER EIGHT: *Wisdom Is Not Enough* 37

PART TWO:
STRATEGY

CHAPTER NINE: *Teams Need Common Purpose* 44

CHAPTER TEN: *Think Like a Chess Player* 49

CHAPTER ELEVEN: *Diversity Is Strength* 53

CHAPTER TWELVE: *Lead Courageously in a Challenging
New World* 58

CHAPTER THIRTEEN: *Corporate Social Responsibility Is
Good Business Strategy* 62

CHAPTER FOURTEEN: *Motivate Your People* 67

CHAPTER FIFTEEN: *Celebrate Entrepreneurship.* 72

CHAPTER SIXTEEN: *Empower and Engage Women* 76

PART THREE:
COMMUNICATION

CHAPTER SEVENTEEN: *Appreciate the Power of Words* 82

CHAPTER EIGHTEEN: *Communicate, Communicate,
Communicate* 86

CHAPTER NINETEEN: *Seek and Provide Honest Feedback* 90

CHAPTER TWENTY: *Take Time to Concentrate* 94

CHAPTER TWENTY-ONE: *Frame the Challenge Correctly* 99

CHAPTER TWENTY-TWO: *Engage in Constructive
Conflict* 104

CHAPTER TWENTY-THREE: *Avoid the Tyranny of
Meetings* 108

CHAPTER TWENTY-FOUR: *Use the Power of Stories* 112

PART FOUR:
RELATIONSHIPS

CHAPTER TWENTY-FIVE: *Great Teams Never Give In* 118

CHAPTER TWENTY-SIX: *Prepare and Adapt As a Team* 122

CHAPTER TWENTY-SEVEN: *Be Generationally Savvy* 126

CHAPTER TWENTY-EIGHT: *Trust and Relationships Matter* 130

CHAPTER TWENTY-NINE: *Cherish the Maverick* 134

CHAPTER THIRTY: *Know Where Power Resides* 138

CHAPTER THIRTY-ONE: *Bring Out the Best In the People Around You* 143

CHAPTER THIRTY-TWO: *Show Humility* 147

PART FIVE:
LEARNING

CHAPTER THIRTY-THREE: *Actively Manage Your Career.* 154

CHAPTER THIRTY-FOUR: *Simplify and Prioritize* 158

CHAPTER THIRTY-FIVE: *Be Present, Listen, and Learn* 162

CHAPTER THIRTY-SIX: *Follow Your Bliss.* 166

CHAPTER THIRTY-SEVEN: *Work Differently* 170

CHAPTER THIRTY-EIGHT: *Succeed In Learning From Failure* 174

CHAPTER THIRTY-NINE: *Recharge Your Batteries* 178

CHAPTER FORTY: *Forge Ahead, For Time Is Precious* 182

Acknowledgments 187

INTRODUCTION

"Life is what happens to you while you're busy making other plans."

– John Lennon

One afternoon in May 2009 my wife, Faith, sat at our kitchen counter reading one of the several local newspapers we receive free of charge at our home in the suburban Twin Cities of Minneapolis and St. Paul. Although I am a great reader of newspapers (I am a terrible *New York Times* and *Wall Street Journal* snob, and I love the *Minneapolis Star Tribune's* sports page), I only occasionally look at those hometown publications. I am lucky that she was taking a peek that day. Life has turned out differently as a result.

Faith shared with me a little blurb that described a new paper called the *Dakota County Tribune Business Weekly* that would be coming out soon in our area south of the Minnesota River. The editor was a fellow named Larry Werner, a long-time newspaper guy who is the general manager and editor of *Thisweek Newspapers* and the *Dakota County Tribune*. Larry was looking for subscribers to the new publication, and for business stories with a local flavor.

I had recently left the Best Buy Co. as part of a generous voluntary severance that Best Buy offered to all its corporate employees. I took the buyout to pursue my passion for history and to continue to build a company that Best Buy had already graciously supported me in starting, Blue Knight History Seminars, LLC. In my business, I take corporate teams out to great American battlefields and create an individual leadership and team-building experience for them. I draw on my knowledge of history but also on a quarter-century of experience as a Marine officer, practicing attorney, corporate executive and entrepreneur. I thought maybe Larry would be interested in doing a little feature on Blue Knight.

When I reached out, Larry went me one better, saying, "How would you like to write a regular column on leadership and teams for the *Business Weekly*?" My answer was enthusiastically affirmative. I wrote the first article that afternoon and sent it off to him. He said he liked it. I told him I thought I could crank one out every two weeks (I was in the midst of writing my first book at the time) and we were in business.

Wisdom Is Not Enough: Reflections on Leadership and Teams is a compilation of forty of the articles I wrote for Larry Werner and the *Dakota County Tribune Business Weekly* over eighteen months from the spring of 2009 to the fall of 2010, during a tremendously difficult time when both the American and world economies struggled mightily. I have divided the book into five parts: "Decision Making," "Strategy," "Communication," "Relationships," and "Learning," with eight chapters in each section.

The essays all explore some facet of leadership or team dynamics but through a wide variety of lenses. Topics range from every type of modern-day business issue, challenge, and story, to the French and Indian War, the journey of Lewis and Clark, the American Civil War, Roald Amundsen's trek to the South Pole, disasters at Mann Gulch, Montana, and high up on Mount Everest, the Cuban Missile Crisis, and the lessons learned from golf and chess. I find that leadership lessons are everywhere if we just look closely enough.

There are a number of key themes that run consistently through all five sections and all forty chapters of the book:

- Great leaders make good decisions. They virtually never have perfect information, but they are tough, smart, and know when to pull the trigger. This is probably the most important — and difficult — thing that leaders get paid to do.

- Great leaders see strategy as the evolution of a compelling common purpose that enables them and their organizations to maintain focus and effectively navigate their way through constantly changing circumstances.

- Great leaders are great communicators. They ensure that their teams understand their message by using multiple channels and erring on the side of overcommunication. They are sensitive to their audience, always honest, and they listen well.

- Great leaders know that nothing is possible without a foundation of strong, trusting relationships. They are sincere in their actions and genuinely care about the people they work and interact with. They spend time creating an environment that values and nurtures talent.

- Great leaders are brutally honest with themselves. They are their own worst critics. They are intense learners, always seeking, always recognizing that someone else may have a better answer than they do. They make constant adjustments and improvements based on what they learn.

- Finally, great leaders think differently, and they foster a diverse culture that permits others to think differently, too. Great leaders understand that the knowledge, skills, and abilities that have worked for them in the past might not work the next time. They know that wisdom is not enough. They are flexible, curious, and willing to try new approaches, even if the result is failure. Because they are great leaders, they will simply pick up, inspire their teams to follow, and try again.

These are the reasons great leaders and the teams they lead are successful. I wish each of you, my readers, great success in your own leadership journey.

– Jeff Appelquist
October 2010

– PART ONE –
DECISION MAKING

"He who has a choice has trouble."

– Danish proverb

— CHAPTER ONE —
GO WITH YOUR GUT - BUT NOT ALWAYS

"Executive: A man who can make quick decisions and is sometimes right."

– Franklin McKinney Hubbard

At first, they believed the fire would be easy to control. In August 1949, fifteen smokejumpers parachuted into a forest fire in a remote area of Montana called Mann Gulch. The situation appeared routine, so much so that the team's leader, Wagner (Wag) Dodge, fed his men and later paused to eat his own dinner before mobilizing to fight the blaze. But circumstances quickly took a perilous turn. The fire accelerated unexpectedly in size and fury, and Wag Dodge suddenly realized that he and his team were in grave danger. He instructed the men to drop their tools in an attempt to outrun the fire, but it spread too rapidly.

In a brilliant flash of intuition, Dodge set a small escape fire in front of the raging inferno, stepped into it, and called to his team to lie down with him in the ashes. The confused and terrified men failed to follow Dodge's lead and instead sprinted frantically to try to stay ahead of the conflagration. Thirteen of the young firefighters perished. Dodge's escape fire, however, had deprived the main blaze of its primary fuel, oxygen, and it swept over and around him as he desperately hugged the earth. He survived unhurt.

In one dramatic instant at Mann Gulch, Wag Dodge demonstrated both the potential benefit and the occasional downside of using intuition in decision making. His hard-won experience told him to set the escape fire that saved his own life, but he failed to save his team. Dodge showed that as a leader, sometimes it is important to go with your gut - but not always.

In his bestselling book *Blink: The Power of Thinking Without Thinking*, author Malcolm Gladwell analyzes this powerful phenomenon of intuitive decision making, of gut-level choices made in a "blink." Gladwell explains that it is the part of our brain known as the adaptive unconscious that enables us to leap to frequently correct conclusions by quickly and efficiently processing huge amounts of data. Indeed, our very survival as human beings depends on our ability to engage in this process of rapid cognition.

Despite our general bias toward thoroughness in decision making - we usually assume that the quality of a decision is in direct proportion to the time and effort that went into making it - Gladwell says, "... decisions made very quickly can be every bit as good as decisions made cautiously and deliberately."

The key to making consistently good intuitive decisions is training and experience. In the case of Wag Dodge, he had spent many more years as a smokejumper than most of the men he led at Mann Gulch. He soon understood the fire was not routine based on pattern recognition from previous fires. His expertise told him that the team could not outrun the fire while carrying their tools and, soon, that they could not outrun the fire at all. While he had never seen an escape fire used before, again, something in his long experience told him that such a technique just might work. He was right, and his men would have survived had they followed his lead. Gladwell says, "This is the gift of training and expertise- the ability to extract an enormous amount of meaningful information from the very thinnest slice of experience."

But it would be foolish for a leader to rely on intuition under every circumstance, for two reasons. First, our instincts can sometimes be disrupted and lead us astray. In other words, sometimes we are wrong. Second, if we rely on gut decisions but fail to communicate our reasoning to our teams and to bring them along - as the Mann Gulch scenario so tragically demonstrates - we will fail in our objectives.

Gladwell writes, "Taking our powers of rapid cognition seriously means we have to acknowledge the subtle influences that can alter or undermine or bias the products of our unconscious." For example, how often do you make a really good decision when you are in an emotional state of mind, frightened, angry or upset? What about decisions made when you are incredibly rushed for time? Self-awareness and open acknowledgment that conditions may not be ideal for a gut-level decision can go a long way toward guiding us to a more deliberative process and a potentially better outcome.

And if our team does not understand what we are doing or why, then we have failed a critical test of leadership as well. For Wag Dodge, a number of important factors worked against him in his effort to make an intuitive decision to save his team. Dodge was generally described as an extremely poor communicator, a man of few words. The team therefore did not know him well to begin with. His team read his actions in taking time to eat his dinner as an indication that all was well. When Dodge quickly discerned that he was wrong in his initial assessment of the fire, he then became pressed for time to convey his urgency to the team. When he called to the men to join him in the escape fire, because they did not know or fully trust him, they could not make sense of his behavior. Disaster resulted.

In the end, we as leaders need to determine when to rely on our intuitive instincts and when to be more thorough in our approach. No two situations are exactly alike and there is no magic formula. Malcolm Gladwell argues that judgment and understanding are critical. He writes, "Judgment matters; it is what separates winners from losers," and, "The key to good decision making is not knowledge. It is understanding. We are swimming in the former. We are desperately lacking in the latter." In using our judgment and understanding, regardless of our decision-making process, we need to communicate effectively to bring our teams with us. The next time you face a critical decision, just remember: Sometimes it is important to go with your gut - but not always.

– CHAPTER TWO –
ASSESS RISK PROPERLY

"If business always made the right decisions, business wouldn't be business."

– J. Paul Getty

I know of a large American company in which the chairman/CEO and president were never allowed to fly together in the corporate jet. The perception was that a plane crash would be devastating to the company from a succession standpoint. However, the pair of them frequently tooled around together in the same automobile. If anyone, including these two very intelligent men, had asked the simple question, "Which is more risky, the plane or the car?" a well-meaning but silly corporate policy might have changed. But we frequently fall short in our ability to determine the relative risk of one activity over another. This inability to estimate and forecast risk correctly can have extremely damaging consequences for our businesses and teams.

In his bestselling book, *Against the Gods: The Remarkable Story of Risk*, author Peter L. Bernstein tells us, "The word 'risk' derives from the early Italian *risicare*, which means 'to dare.' In this sense, risk is a choice, rather than a fate. The actions we dare to take, which depend on how free we are to make choices, are what the story of risk is all about. And that story helps define what it means to be a human being."

Bernstein further explains that "when the growth of trade transformed the principles of gambling into the creation of wealth, the inevitable result was capitalism, the epitome of risk-taking." But he argues capitalism could only flourish with the development of two new concepts: bookkeeping, which allowed for the quantification and tracking of business results, and forecasting, which is a "challenging activity that links risk-taking with direct payoffs." Indeed, in Bernstein's view, "The successful business executive is a forecaster first; purchasing, producing, marketing, pricing, and organizing all follow." In other words, the best business leaders are those who are especially adept at properly assessing risk.

Nevertheless, obstacles come in many forms, even for the most skillful forecasters. In a classic *Harvard Business Review* article from 1998 entitled, "The Hidden Traps in Decision Making," scholars John S. Hammond, Ralph L. Keeney and Howard Raiffa describe three common traps that affect the quality of our assessments and predictions about uncertain events.

First, leaders succumb to the "overconfidence trap." Human beings are generally not very good at estimating the outcome of uncertain events, yet we have a strong tendency to overestimate our own abilities. This phenomenon is nicely summarized by Stanford professor James G. March in his book, *A Primer on Decision Making: How Decisions Happen*. March says, "Decision makers tend to exaggerate their control over their environment, overweighting the impacts of their actions and underweighting the impact of other factors, including chance. They believe things happen because of their intentions and their skills... more than because of contributions from the environment. This tendency is accentuated by success. As a result... there is a strong tendency to treat uncertainty as something to be removed rather than estimated."

The second pitfall is the "prudence trap," which describes the very natural human tendency to be overcautious when faced with a risky and important decision. The *HBR* article cites the example of a Big Three U.S. automaker that, in anticipation of extremely high sales volume, collected forecasts from various departments that each overestimated the number of cars that should be produced, "just to be on the safe side." The cumulative effect of the prudence trap for this organization was gross overproduction and excess inventory that eventually had to be sold at reduced prices.

The final obstacle is the "recallability trap," which results from our strong tendency to recall and be overly influenced by dramatic events from our past in making predictions about the future. The *HBR* article says, "We all, for example, exaggerate the probability of rare but catastrophic occurrences such as plane crashes because they get disproportionate attention in the media."

We also tend to possess a skewed memory about the frequency of various events. Professor March explains, "Decision makers tend to overlook important information about the base rates of events. Even though the greatest hitters in history were successful only about 40 percent of the time in their best seasons, there is a tendency to expect great baseball hitters to hit whenever they bat, because hitting is what is prototypical of great hitters. Similarly, although great designers produce exceptional designs only a few times in a lifetime, every failure of a great designer to produce a great design is experienced as surprise."

What can you do as a business leader to improve your ability to properly assess risk?

- Ability to overcome obstacles starts with the recognition that obstacles exist. Simple awareness of such tendencies as the overconfidence, prudence, and recallability traps in all of us, including capable and experienced leaders, represents the first step. Recognizing that you might fall prey to these pitfalls in your decision making goes a long way toward enabling you to consciously avoid them.

- Challenge your own assumptions, especially when you feel confident that you are right. Ask yourself which incidents from your past are influencing your present decision. Seek information and input from many sources, especially when a high-risk decision is at stake. Ask peers and subordinates for their estimates and challenge them as well.

- Use facts in making your assessments. Don't rely on stories or anecdotes, but use hard data.

- When confronted with information that puts into question or even directly contradicts your own point of view, be open to the new input. Analyze your options honestly and with a willingness to be proven wrong.

With these steps, the probability that you will become a more skilled business forecaster is high. Your odds will never be perfect, but with hard work and sensitivity to obstacles, I predict great things for you and your team.

– CHAPTER THREE –
COLLABORATE EFFECTIVELY IN DECISION MAKING

"None of us is as smart as all of us."

– Warren Bennis

The Battle of Gettysburg was the largest battle ever fought in the Western Hemisphere and a critical turning point in the American Civil War. The second day of the battle, July 2, 1863, was one of the bloodiest in American history, with approximately 20,000 combined casualties (killed, wounded, missing or captured). As evening slowly gave way to night at the end of that terrible day, General George Gordon Meade, commander of the Union Army of the Potomac, called his entire leadership team together at his headquarters for a council of war. Meade knew in his own mind the outcome he desired on the battle's third day, but he also wanted to hear from his commanders and to achieve consensus regarding the Union strategy for the endgame. Meade instinctively understood the critical need, at this dramatic moment in time, to collaborate effectively in decision making.

Meade and his counterpart, the extremely capable Robert E. Lee, commanding general of the Confederate Army of Northern Virginia, were locked in mortal combat. Several weeks earlier, Lee had begun an invasion of Northern territory and the two mighty armies had met accidentally, but with unspeakable fury, at the little cross-roads borough of Gettysburg in south central Pennsylvania. By the end of the second day, after much desperate fighting, the armies lay in stalemate, watching each other warily across contested ground like two wounded but still very dangerous animals.

General Meade had established his headquarters in a tiny white farmhouse owned by the widow Lydia Leister. Earlier on July 2 he had wired his superiors in Washington, D.C., to let them know it was his intention to "remain in my present position tomorrow..." Nevertheless, that night he gathered his top generals (eleven in all) to listen to their assessment of the situation. They assembled in a room no larger than twelve by twelve feet, illuminated by a single candle, and which was soon filled with a thick cloud of cigar smoke.

The discussion began informally, and turned to the issues of the dire condition of the army and the lack of supplies. Meade was quiet, offering only an occasional comment, and intent on hearing what his team had to say before offering his own judgment. Finally, with Meade's concurrence, his chief of staff proposed that the group vote on three critical questions: 1. Should the army remain in its present position? 2. If the army remains, should it attack or await the enemy's attack? 3. If the decision is to await attack, how long should it wait? After much give and take, the generals voted unanimously to stay in their present position, await attack, and to wait for not much longer than a day.

One of the participants, General John Gibbon, wrote afterward, "I recollect there was great good feeling amongst the Corp Commanders at their agreeing so unanimously, and Gen. Meade announced, in a decided manner, 'Such then is the decision.'" The generals left the meeting clear in the understanding of their mission and united in their common purpose to defeat the enemy the next day, which they succeeded in doing. This stroke of genius — attaining clarity and consensus during a critical phase of the fight — on the part of George Meade may have (more than anything else he did over the three days) won the Battle of Gettysburg for the North.

What can modern-day business leaders learn from the historical example of Meade's collaborative decision making? First, Meade recognized the criticality of pulling his team together for a face-to-face consultation. Sometimes, there is simply no substitute for a meeting in person, and skilled leaders understand precisely when there is a need to bring everyone into the same room. Ironically, Meade's adversary General Lee did not gather his commanding generals together for a war council at any point during the battle, and a serious lack of coordination resulted.

Next, Meade initiated a process that was perceived by all of the participants as fair. While it is true that Meade had already indicated to higher command his preference for remaining in place, he did not disclose his point of view to those reporting to him. Instead, he remained quiet and listened respectfully with genuine interest to what the others had to say. Each person had a chance to weigh in on the discussion and to vote on a particular outcome. When the members of a team feel that they have been given ample opportunity to express their points of view and to influence their leader, even if they disagree with the final decision, they are much more inclined to buy into the ultimate direction.

Finally, Meade's council of war provided absolute clarity to every individual involved as to what was expected of him for the next day. The fact that the decisions made were unanimous helped in achieving this effect but, even if there had been disagreement, the rationale for the chosen decision was clear and unambiguous.

On the morning of July 3, after the famous meeting but before the decisive combat that would bring victory to his forces, Meade penned a hurried letter to his wife: "Dearest love, All well and going on well with the Army. We had a great fight yesterday, the enemy attacking and we completely repulsing them — both armies shattered.... Army in fine spirits and every one determined to do or die." This determination to defeat the Confederate enemy at all costs was in large part achieved as a result of George Meade's intuitive comprehension of the importance of effective collaboration when making a critical decision.

– CHAPTER FOUR –
USE THE RIGHT DATA

"Facts are available to everyone; it is interpretation and implementation that is key."

– Ric Simcock

Some of the most serious and prevalent problems that plague modern business result from using the wrong data to make decisions, measure outcomes, and incent performance. Recently, business journalist Geoff Colvin wrote, "In business as in life, be careful what you wish for. I know a company that wished for a better return on equity. What could be wrong with that? It paid its executives according to that measure, and man, did they deliver. In some years the firm had the best ROE in the industry. It was winning big time. The firm was Lehman Brothers, now dead because managing for ROE caused executives to overborrow.... Wishing for the wrong thing — managing for the wrong ratio — killed the company."

The cautionary tale of Lehman Brothers is just one among many to come out of the Great Recession. These days, smart business leaders are meticulously careful to use the right data.

We are obsessed by numbers and have become increasingly good at measuring all manner of things. The July-August 2009 issue of *Harvard Business Review* states, "Data, computing power, and mathematical models have been transforming many realms of management from art to science. But the crisis exposed the limitations of certain tools. In particular, the world saw the folly of reliance by banks, insurance companies, and others on financial models that assumed economic rationality, linearity, equilibrium, and bell-curve distribution. As the recession unfolded, it became clear that the models had failed badly."

The measurement tools and models are not in and of themselves necessarily flawed. Business leaders simply need to become more adept at comprehending and utilizing effectively the data they generate. *HBR* argues, ".... decision makers in every industry must take responsibility for looking inside the black boxes that advanced quantitative tools often represent and understanding their functioning, assumptions, and limitations."

Consider the incredibly controversial issue of executive and, specifically, CEO compensation. Duke University business professor Dan Ariely points out that numerous studies demonstrate that people will behave based upon whatever measures we use to evaluate them. It seems too simple to contemplate but, says Ariely, "Human beings adjust behavior based on the metrics they're held up against. Anything you measure will impel a person to optimize his score on that metric. What you measure is what you get. Period."

Chief executives are overwhelmingly evaluated based on a single data point: the value of their company's stock. Even measuring CEOs against several years' worth of stock returns does not necessarily incent them to consider the long-term health of the enterprise they lead — they are still obsessed by stock price. It is not surprising, therefore, that because they are primarily compensated based on that one measure, most CEOs spend an inordinate amount of time considering and working towards an improved stock price.

Professor Ariely says, "To change CEOs' behavior, we need to change the numbers we measure. Stock value metrics that focus on the long term are a start, but even more important are new numbers that direct leaders' attention to the real drivers of sustainable success. What are those numbers? …. How many new jobs have been created at your firm? How strong is your pipeline of new patents? How satisfied are your customers? Your employees? What's the level of trust in your company and brand? How much carbon dioxide do you emit?"

Geoff Colvin asserts that businesses should evaluate performance using a new metric, called "EVA momentum." Economic value added, or EVA (a measure used by some companies), is essentially net profit after the subtraction of costs for all the various factors of production. An improvement in EVA presumably results in increased value, yet some business thinkers believe EVA can still be manipulated and is not a fool-proof metric. EVA momentum is defined as the change in EVA divided by the prior period's sales and, the argument goes, simply cannot be tinkered with. Consultant Bennett Stewart says in referring to EVA momentum, "It's the only performance metric where more is always better than less. It always increases when managers do things that make economic sense."

Even at the level of macroeconomics and public policy we see much current discussion about the data that informs decision making. Nobel prize-winning economists Joseph Stiglitz and Amartya Sen produced a recent study that blames the disproportionate focus on growth in the form of gross domestic product (the quantity of goods and services produced in the economy) for contributing to the world-wide recession. An unhealthy fixation on G.D.P. causes governments to overlook such problems as joblessness and environmental degradation, which are also important quantifiers of the overall health of the economy. Stiglitz says, "If you don't measure the right thing, you don't do the right thing," and he advocates for more attention on such benchmarks as income and consumption, availability of health care, and quality of education.

Temple University mathematics professor John Allen Paulos wrote an article recently in the *New York Times Magazine* called, "Metric Mania: Do we expect too much from our data?" Dr. Paulos says, "In the realm of public policy, we live in an age of numbers.... The problem isn't with statistical tests themselves but with what we do before and after we run them." He argues that measures in such areas as school performance and health care can be second-guessed, but that, "This doesn't mean we shouldn't be counting.... It does mean we should do so with as much care and wisdom as we can muster."

Albert Einstein supposedly said, "Not everything that can be counted counts, and not everything that counts can be counted." What measures do you use in your business to make decisions, assess performance, and reward behaviors? Are you careful and wise in your use of data, or do you rely on certain metrics just because you've "always done it that way"? The answers to these critical questions are essential to the future success of your business.

– CHAPTER FIVE –
BE AWARE OF COGNITIVE ROADBLOCKS TO GOOD DECISION MAKING

"It is a common fault of men not to reckon on storms in fair weather."

– Niccolo Machiavelli

In May 1996, two commercial expeditions consisting of participants who paid up to $65,000 each to be professionally guided to the summit of Mount Everest (the world's tallest peak) became trapped in a blizzard high on the mountain. This tragic event was immortalized in Jon Krakauer's famous best-seller, *Into Thin Air*. (Krakauer, a journalist, accompanied one of the expeditions.) Two of the world's best-known and most experienced mountaineers, Scott Fischer and Rob Hall, served as expedition leaders.

In addition to the financial outlay, the effort to reach the summit of Everest requires a huge time commitment; climbers must spend six weeks acclimatizing their bodies to the high altitude. Over this period of time, the two teams established a series of base camps at ever-increasing heights, and then finally embarked on an arduous, 18-hour round-trip to reach the summit. During the climb, an unexpected and violent storm quickly struck the mountain. Fischer, Hall, and three other climbers all lost their lives.

Perhaps the most important skill of an effective leader is the ability to make good decisions. Yet as human beings we are susceptible to cognitive biases that can hinder the decision-making process. The word "cognitive" refers to the mental acquisition of knowledge through thought, experience, and the senses. A cognitive bias is simply a distortion in our perception of reality that can occur when we use traditional shortcuts to help us make choices. Most of the time, these shortcuts allow us to arrive efficiently at a good decision.

Sometimes, however, making choices in the most economical manner based on familiar rules of thumb is not the right thing to do. Even competent, knowledgeable, and experienced leaders can get caught up in this trap. Because we are human, we will never completely overcome our natural biases, but we can learn to make better choices by simply being aware of cognitive roadblocks to good decision making.

Cognitive biases can take many forms, but in the case of the Mount Everest tragedy of 1996, three types of bias contributed significantly to the disaster:

- The overconfidence bias
- The sunk-cost or escalation of commitment bias
- The recency effect

In a pamphlet entitled, *The Art of Critical Decision Making*, Professor Michael Roberto of Bryant University elaborates on the cognitive biases that reared their ugly heads to contribute to the Everest disaster.

First, Roberto explains, "the expedition leaders clearly displayed evidence of the overconfidence bias." Research shows that human beings have a consistent tendency to be overly optimistic. For example, studies indicate that even experienced physicians tend to be unrealistically positive in their diagnoses. In talking about Everest, Scott Fischer said, "We've got the Big E completely figured out, we've got it totally wired. These days, I'm telling you, we've built a yellow brick road to the summit." Other members of the team became cocky as well. Jon Krakauer described several of the highly inexperienced amateur climbers as so overconfident in their own abilities as to be "clinically delusional."

The second cognitive bias is the sunk-cost effect. A rational actor makes choices based on the marginal cost of pursuing one choice over another. In contrast, the sunk-cost effect causes people to continue in a sometimes catastrophic course of action in which they have invested significant time, money and/or effort. On Everest, expedition members refused to allow their huge financial expenditure and many weeks of herculean effort to be for nothing. With the blessing of their leaders, they pushed ahead to the summit, blatantly in violation of well-established turnaround times. A number of climbers reached the top too late in the afternoon, and were forced to descend the mountain while negotiating a furious storm in the dark.

Another common term for this same basic phenomenon is the

escalation of commitment bias. Consider America's experience in Vietnam, or the current debate about Afghanistan. We have spent eight hard years fighting in that troubled country at great cost in blood and treasure. To be sure, all of our choices there are tough ones. Yet the argument still centers not on whether we should withdraw, pursue a different strategy, or otherwise cut our losses, but rather at what level we will continue the effort.

The final cognitive bias is the recency effect, which simply refers to the tendency to place a disproportionate value on information obtained recently. This newer data becomes salient to us, and can cause us to overlook other relevant information. On Everest, team leaders were fooled by their experience of a recent string of years in which good weather had prevailed on the mountain. One commentator said, "Season after season, Rob [Hall] had brilliant weather on summit day. He'd never been caught in a storm high on the mountain." No one prepared for the worst case scenario. Calamity resulted because of this failure on the part of leadership to consider ample data that for many years in the more distant past, deadly storms had been a common occurrence on Everest.

Think about your own decision making as a business leader. Have you ever allowed overconfidence, sunk-costs, or recency to sway your mind one way or the other? Don't be too hard on yourself if the answer is yes. Despite what some economists would have us believe, none of us are perfectly rational actors. We all occasionally yield to a lifetime of biases. Nevertheless, we can improve our decision making if we develop the self-knowledge to be aware of these tendencies and, wherever possible, to overcome them.

– CHAPTER SIX –
SMALL DECISIONS MATTER

"The doors we open and close each day decide the lives we live."

– Flora Whittemore

By the year 1759 Great Britain and France had been locked in a 150-year struggle for control of the North American continent. A series of smaller wars had preceded the great world-wide conflict that erupted in 1756, known in Europe as the Seven Years' War and in America as the French and Indian War. In September 1759 a combined British invasion force of naval vessels and foot soldiers, under the command of the youthful but determined General James Wolfe, stood poised to capture the mighty French fortress city of Quebec, in Canada.

Quebec held a geographic position that was the key to the control of the St. Lawrence River; the extensive reach of the St. Lawrence was in turn essential to anyone seeking the dominance of all of Canada. The outcome of the upcoming epic battle would determine the future of North America. In that battle, an apparently small decision made at the middle levels of the British army had a huge impact on the ultimate result. In history, in business, and in life, seemingly inconsequential decisions often have profound repercussions. No decision should be taken lightly, therefore, because sometimes even small decisions matter.

General Wolfe and his 8,500-man army had been attempting to capture Quebec for nearly three months. The walled city sat high on the bluffs above the St. Lawrence and was ably defended by French and allied forces under the command of General Louis-Joseph, marquis de Montcalm. To the west of the city were high, steep cliffs that were most likely impossible to climb. But after attempting to engage the French and overtake the fortress by every other means, Wolfe gambled that his troops could scale the heights to the level ground above (called the Plains of Abraham) using a narrow, sheer, mostly hidden footpath. Wolfe would then attack the enemy on the open terrain from the west.

At four o'clock in the morning of September 13, 1759, having disembarked from landing boats that floated downriver quietly in the dark, General Wolfe and 200 members of his advance guard struggled up the secret path. They seized the lightly guarded position atop the bluffs, but in the resulting confusion and a nearly catastrophic moment of hesitation, Wolfe sent word to the officer below, who was supervising the landing, to halt the flow of men up the path. Fortunately for the British cause that officer, Major Isaac Barre, made a seemingly small decision by disregarding Wolfe's order. Major Barre continued to send infantry en masse in a rush up the precipice. By dawn, 4,800 determined British soldiers were in position to confront the French upon the Plains of Abraham.

In the ensuing fighting, both Wolfe and Montcalm were killed, but the British emerged triumphant. The victory ultimately allowed England to win the war and secure control of the continent. James Wolfe is regarded as a great hero of British history, but without the small decision of an obscure mid-level officer to ignore Wolfe's foolish order, the outcome of the battle for Quebec may have been different, and those of us in America who speak English today might well be speaking French instead.

Small decisions matter in business and careers as well. On April Fools' Day in 1976, three men — Steve Jobs, Steve Wozniak, and Ron Wayne — founded Apple Computer Inc. Who is Ron Wayne, you ask? The youthful Jobs and Wozniak asked the older and more experienced Wayne to be their partner at Apple, with a 10 percent stake in the company. Wayne's most important responsibility was to mediate disputes between the two strong-headed principle owners. He designed the original Apple logo, drafted the Apple 1 computer manual, and wrote the initial partnership agreement. But he soon became concerned with Jobs's extravagant spending and Wozniak's occasionally weird thinking. After twelve days, out of fear that he was the only member of the partnership with actual assets that creditors could seize, Wayne sold back his share of the company for $800. His 10 percent ownership stake would today be worth $22 billion.

To his credit, Wayne does not spend much time lamenting his decision. He says, "I left Apple for reasons that seemed sound to me at the time. Why should I go back now and 'what if' myself? If I did, I'd be in a rubber room by now." But he also observes, "My whole life has been a day late and a dollar short." Because of an apparently small decision that turned out poorly, Ron Wayne's name is but an interesting footnote in the annals of one of the world's richest, most highly respected corporations.

Small decisions matter in life, too. On April Fools' Day in 1984, eight years to the day after the original Apple partnership was formed, I spotted a pretty young woman across a crowded room in a watering hole on State Street in Madison, where I was attending graduate school at the University of Wisconsin. We exchanged glances and a smile, but, eventually, she got up to put on her coat and leave. I had a decision to make. Should I talk to her? Or should I let her go? I was genuinely at a loss, and the issue might have gone either way. It was really a close call. I finally summoned all my courage and waved her over to my table. She sat down, and I learned that her name was Faith (go figure). In less than two weeks, we will celebrate our twenty-fifth wedding anniversary.

My friends, please trust me when I tell you that small decisions matter.

– CHAPTER SEVEN –
DEVELOP A DECISION-MAKING PROCESS

"Good decisions come from experience, and experience comes from bad decisions."

– Unknown

Soon after his inauguration as U.S. president in January 1961, John F. Kennedy received a briefing concerning a CIA plan to invade Cuba. The island of Cuba sits only 90 miles from U.S. territory and the deeply anti-American Communist dictator Fidel Castro had just seized power in 1959. During the late stages of the Eisenhower administration, the CIA undertook an effort to train Cuban exiles in Guatemala for purposes of invading Cuba and overthrowing the Castro regime. Eisenhower approved of the plan but his term in office expired before the invasion could take place. Kennedy inherited the proposal and, despite his grave doubts about its potential for success, directed his subordinates to continue to flesh out the initiative.

The subsequent invasion of Cuba at the infamous Bay of Pigs was a tragic fiasco that historian Theodore Draper later described as "one of those rare events in history: a perfect failure." That perfect failure resulted in significant part because neither President Kennedy nor his advisors had taken the time to develop an effective decision-making process. But Kennedy learned from this painful early set-back, and put into place better methodologies that allowed him to save the world from disaster later in his administration during the thirteen tension-filled days known as the Cuban Missile Crisis.

A number of serious flaws characterized the decision-making process that led to the Bay of Pigs debacle. First, there never appeared to be any serious consideration of an alternative to invasion. The planning process revolved entirely around the details and timing of the attack, which came to be presumed as inevitable. Second, certain individuals who had serious concerns about the plan either failed to aggressively articulate those concerns, were marginalized for their dissenting views, or were left out of the deliberations entirely.

Finally, miscommunication and misinformation plagued the process from the very beginning. For example, planners believed the invasion would prompt a massive internal anti-Castro uprising within Cuba, which it did not. Additionally, the CIA and the Joint Chiefs of Staff assumed that if the operation failed at the beaches, President Kennedy would intervene with U.S. military power, which in reality Kennedy had no intention of ever doing.

In his fine biography entitled *An Unfinished Life: John F. Kennedy, 1917-1963*, presidential scholar Robert Dallek writes, "[advisor Arthur] Schlesinger asked JFK, 'What do you think about this damned invasion?' Kennedy replied, 'I think about it as little as possible,' implying that it was too painful a subject with too many uncertainties for him to dwell on it. But of course it was at the center of his concerns."

On April 17, 1961, 1,400 Cuban exiles hit the beach at the Bay of Pigs. Lacking additional military support from the U.S. and greatly outmanned and outgunned by Castro's soldiers, all of the invaders were either killed or captured. To his credit, Kennedy fully accepted blame for the tragedy, telling the nation, "I am the responsible officer of the government." Nevertheless, U.S. prestige had been badly damaged and the young, inexperienced president was seen as weak and lacking in resolve, particularly by his adversary Soviet Premier Nikita Khrushchev.

In the spring of 1962 Khrushchev and his military commanders hatched a plan to install forty nuclear warheads, as well as to deploy thousands of support troops and build a Soviet naval base on the island of Cuba. One of his advisors wrote later that the Bay of Pigs "gave Khrushchev and the other leaders the impression that Kennedy was indecisive." Unfortunately for the Soviet premier, Kennedy and team had taken the excruciating lessons of the Bay of Pigs to heart and succeeded in putting a vastly more disciplined decision-making process into place.

Upon learning with certainty of the presence of Soviet missiles in Cuba in October 1962, Kennedy formed a team of key advisors called the Executive Committee (ExComm) that met frequently over thirteen days to debate the new challenge.

ExComm and President Kennedy performed in an exemplary way that is instructive to business leaders even today. The team considered a number of options, not just one preordained choice, and finally narrowed the decision to either a military air strike or the more conservative tactic of a naval blockade of Cuba. The team broke into two groups to develop and articulate these two options. Experts were invited to speak up, not just on the topic of their expertise, but on any aspect of the deliberations. Kennedy encouraged dissent and an honest airing of differences of opinion. He sought independent advice on his own outside of his immediate team. ExComm did not focus on hierarchy of rank, and members treated each other as equals. Kennedy himself skipped some of the meetings to allow his advisors to brainstorm without him in the room; also, the president did not tip his hand in terms of which way he leaned in the discussion.

In the end, Kennedy opted for the naval blockade and, as the world held its breath, Khrushchev backed down and withdrew his missiles from Cuba. Kennedy's team, and indeed the entire world, had benefited from an open, inclusive, and thorough decision-making process.

Robert Dallek summarizes, "Forty years after the crisis, historians almost uniformly agree that this was the most dangerous moment in the forty-five year Cold War. Moreover…. they generally have high praise for Kennedy's performance. His restraint in resisting a military solution that would almost certainly have triggered a nuclear exchange makes him a model of wise statesmanship in a dire situation…. October 1962 was not only Kennedy's finest hour in the White House; it was also an imperishable example of how one man prevented a catastrophe that may yet afflict the world."

– CHAPTER EIGHT –
WISDOM IS NOT ENOUGH

"Old ways of thinking, old formulas, dogmas, and ideologies, no matter how cherished or how useful in the past, no longer fit the facts."

– Alvin Toffler

As he worked feverishly in his Washington, D.C., office to avoid economic catastrophe during the Great Recession of 2007-2009, Federal Reserve Chairman Ben Bernanke looked up from his desk from time to time at a portrait of four men on the wall. These four men, Montague Norman of Great Britain, Emile Moreau of France, Hjalmar Schacht of Germany, and Benjamin Strong of the United States, served as the central bankers for their respective nations prior to the Great Depression of 1929-1933. For Bernanke, the portrait served as a grim reminder that despite good intentions, intelligence, and experience, sometimes leaders fail to recognize that times have changed and that they must adjust their actions accordingly. For Bernanke, the picture on the wall reinforced the simple but powerful leadership principle that sometimes, wisdom is not enough.

In his book, *Lords of Finance: The Bankers Who Broke the World*, author Liaquat Ahamed argues that the Great Depression came about not through events beyond human control but primarily as a result of poor decision making by the four influential central bankers, Norman, Moreau, Schacht and Strong. Ahamed writes, "I maintain that the Great Depression was not some act of God or the result of some deep-rooted contradictions of capitalism but the direct result of a series of misjudgments by economic policy makers, some made back in the 1920s, others after the first crises set in, by any measure the most dramatic sequence of collective blunders ever made by financial officials."

At the height of the Depression, economic misery ran rampant throughout the world. One quarter of the eligible population in the major economies was jobless, with wages for those who remained employed down by one third. Real gross domestic product declined by more than 25 percent and consumer prices fell by 30 percent. Bank credit dried up and some countries realized the collapse of their entire banking systems. The effects of this terrible situation eventually set the stage for the rise to power of Adolf Hitler and Nazi Germany.

While Ahamed rightly identifies the politicians who convened at the Paris Peace Conference after the First World War as having made a number of short-sighted choices — most notably, burdening defeated Germany with unrealistic war reparations — he heaps most of the blame for setting the world on a path to disaster on the central bankers. In particular, these four men, brilliant, knowledgeable, and well-meaning though they might have been, all agreed and labored tirelessly to return the world to the gold standard which had prevailed prior to the war. Unfortunately, this solution represented a wishful effort to turn back the clock to an era that no longer existed. A return to gold was highly impractical because gold bullion now resided disproportionately in the United States and prices had far outstripped the supply of gold.

In addition, the central bankers feared inflation above all else, and worked to keep interest rates low in the U.S. while simultaneously propping up Germany with borrowed money. In the end, they could accomplish neither of these misguided goals, and the system came crashing down. Ahamed says, "To reestablish sanity and restore some sort of equilibrium in these circumstances required a very visible head to guide the invisible hand. In a word, it required leadership.... responsibility for world monetary affairs ended up in the hands of a group of men who understood none of this, whose ideas about the economy were at best outmoded and at worst plain wrong."

Flash forward to the current crisis and Ben Bernanke (who cites *Lords of Finance* as one of his favorite books). Despite his extremely vocal critics (many people hold Bernanke and the Fed directly responsible for the current debacle through lax oversight) *Time* magazine honored Bernanke as the Person of the Year for 2009, saying, ".... he is the most important player guiding the world's most important economy. His creative leadership helped ensure that 2009 was a period of weak recovery rather than catastrophic depression, and he still wields unrivaled power over our money, our jobs, our savings and our national future."

Indeed, Bernanke sits uniquely positioned to head up the Federal Reserve at this moment in our history. He is a scholar of economics with a special expertise in the lessons of the Great Depression, which he calls "the holy grail of macroeconomics." His view is that the effort to tighten belts and balance budgets during the Depression was exactly the wrong response. He takes the position that only aggressive government action and an immense infusion of public money can restore confidence and create demand.

Bernanke is the first to acknowledge that he did not see the crisis coming but, once it came, he sprang into action. *Time* says, "He.... made a conscious decision to avoid the mistakes made by the bankers of the 1930s — not only their stingy refusals to supply cash but also their inflexible inside-the-box thinking.... He held 'blue sky' brainstorming sessions to solicit unorthodox ideas."

While only time will reveal the ultimate outcome of Bernanke's approach, there is general consensus that we are clearly better off for his actions than we might otherwise have been. Ben Bernanke provides a great example of a leader who recognizes that intelligence and experience alone are not sufficient in today's complex world, and that new ways of thinking are required to solve our problems.

As a leader, do you hold onto ideas that are "at best outmoded and at worst plain wrong"? Most of us have a very strong inclination to rely on knowledge, experience, and methodologies that have worked for us in the past. Perhaps the best defense against orthodox and stale thinking is to simply recognize this very human tendency, and to acknowledge when we see it in ourselves. The next time you find yourself going down an old familiar decision-making path and coming up dissatisfied with the results, check your thought processes and your approach. Remember, wisdom is not enough.

– Part Two –
Strategy

"All men can see these tactics whereby I conquer, but what none can see is the strategy out of which victory is evolved."

– Sun Tzu

– CHAPTER NINE –
TEAMS NEED COMMON PURPOSE

"Companies that enjoy enduring success have core values and a core purpose that remain fixed while their business strategies and practices endlessly adapt to a changing world."

– Jim Collins

In the early stages of the Vietnam War, U.S. Navy pilot James Bond Stockdale was shot down over enemy territory and captured. For more than seven years, from 1965 to 1973, Commander (later Admiral) Stockdale was the highest-ranking prisoner-of-war (POW) at the Hoa Lo Camp, otherwise known as the Hanoi Hilton, in the capital city of North Vietnam. He endured torture and deprivation beyond imagination during his long years of imprisonment. But James Stockdale also valiantly led his fellow POWs throughout their shared ordeal with great imagination and courage, helping the vast majority of them to survive their time in captivity physically and psychologically intact. Stockdale used a variety of leadership techniques but, above all else, his team prevailed because he provided them with a common purpose.

In 1981, Stockdale gave a commencement address to the graduates of John Carroll University, in which he summarized the essence of his leadership during the time at Hoa Lo: "From this eight-year experience, I distilled one all-purpose idea.... it is a simple idea.... an idea that naturally and spontaneously comes to men under pressure.... You are your brother's keeper."

In an article about Stockdale from the November 2009 issue of *Proceedings* (a publication of the U.S. Naval Institute), authors Peter Fretwell and Taylor Baldwin Kiland write, "Any organization that articulates a purposeful goal in front of its members has started building a culture in which individuality can support solidarity, and in which personal desires (especially those of top management) take a backseat to the common good."

This powerful concept that the well-being of the whole team was more important than the plight of any one individual, described by Stockdale as "Unity over Self," was the compelling common purpose that allowed a disparate group of individuals to remain a cohesive team in an incredibly challenging environment.

Stockdale confronted mighty obstacles in leading his fellow prisoners. First, the men were physically separated, with no ability to communicate directly. Stockdale developed a communication strategy involving a wall tap code and other means of secret messaging which allowed him to continually lead and encourage his team despite their isolation.

Next, the team consisted of hundreds of individuals from very diverse backgrounds and experiences. Fretwell and Kiland write, "The POWs were not a case study in conformity. Knowing this, Stockdale harnessed the diversity and gave them latitude. And in their common purpose, he also held out hope and solidarity." Stockdale, knowing that he had no capacity to micromanage the situation — even if he wanted to — succeeded in communicating the compelling central idea of "Unity over Self" that sustained itself among the soldiers and sailors he led over a period of many years.

Finally, Stockdale's men faced loneliness, deprivation and torture on a daily basis. Stockdale provided very precise guidelines on how the men were to act under duress. He wrote later, "We organized a clandestine society.... with our own laws, traditions, customs, even heroes. [This explains how we could].... order each other into more torture.... refuse to comply with specific demands, [and] intentionally call the bluff of our jailers...." Stockdale succeeded in creating a cohesive culture with ironclad and widely known rules which perpetuated itself and provided motivation and discipline to its members even under the most difficult of circumstances.

Of the 591 Hanoi Hilton POWs who returned safely, almost 80 percent remained in the military, with 24 of them advancing to the rank of general or admiral. A significant number of the returnees became leaders in business, law, government or politics. Fully 96 percent of the former prisoners were free of any symptoms of posttraumatic stress disorder, a remarkable statistic considering that better than half of a small group of American POWs studied from World War II and Korea suffered from long-term mental illness. James Stockdale's brilliant and inspirational leadership went a long way toward ensuring that the men in his charge would return home to pursue healthy, productive lives.

How can this amazing story translate into a meaningful lesson for today's business leaders? Wilson Learning conducted a survey in 2006 of 25,000 workers in finance and high tech who asserted overwhelmingly that they needed a leader who could "convey clearly what the work unit is trying to do." This is an incredibly simple proposition, but many leaders fail the test.

In a recent interview in the *New York Times*, Ford Motor CEO Alan Mulally states, "...the biggest thing I've found is that the more that everybody comes together on what their real purpose is, the higher order of that, the better.... And so the higher the calling, the higher the compelling vision that you can articulate, the more it pulls everybody in."

For former CEO Jack Welch of General Electric, strategy was not a lengthy action plan but rather the evolution of a central idea through continuously changing circumstances (think again of Stockdale's "Unity over Self" concept). For Welch, the central idea was that GE would be "number one or number two in all of our businesses, or else we will fix, sell, or close that business." Welch repeated this mantra over and over during his very successful twenty-year tenure and all of his employees, like it or not, knew their common purpose.

Have you as a leader provided your team with a common purpose? Do team members understand and can they articulate that purpose? What is the central idea that drives your organization forward, through good times and bad? If you are fuzzy on these answers, you can bet your team is confused as well. Now is the time to step up and, with confidence and conviction, "convey what the work unit is trying to do." You will be amazed at the results that clarity of purpose can produce.

– CHAPTER TEN –
THINK LIKE A CHESS PLAYER

"Life is like a game of Chess, changing with each move."

– Chinese Proverb

The game of chess is a metaphor for business, and for life. Seemingly simple at the most basic level, chess is in reality mind-boggling in its complexity. The focus, discipline, and skill required to play chess well are reminiscent of the same attributes that are required to succeed in business. While not every business leader plays chess, every business leader can benefit from thinking like a chess player.

I first became fascinated by chess as a youngster in the early 1970s when the quirky American prodigy Bobby Fisher defeated the reigning world champion, the Russian Boris Spassky, in their famous title match in Reykjavik, Iceland. My sister and I played chess for hours on end. While there have been periods when I studied and played intensively, I have never been better than an average player, but I still love the game.

In his wonderful book, *The Immortal Game: A History of Chess, or How 32 Carved Pieces on a Board Illuminated Our Understanding of War, Art, Science and the Human Brain*, author David Shenk says, "The exquisite interplay of the simple and the complex is hypnotic:

the pieces and moves are elementary enough for any five-year-old to quickly soak up, but the board combinations are so vast that all the possible chess games could never be played — or even known — by a single person."

Indeed, in any chess game, after just four moves by each player, the number of possible board positions is 315 billion. Shenk says, "The total number of unique chess games is not literally an infinite number, but in practical terms, the difference is indistinguishable. It is truly beyond comprehension — 'barely thinkable,' as one expert puts it — and beyond human or machine capacity to play through them all."

Business, like chess, can be seemingly elementary on its surface. The *Oxford English Dictionary* defines business simply as "commercial activity." Those of us who are in business know that our most fundamental objective is to sell our product or services to customers at a profit. It's easy, right? Actually, it isn't. Because when we delve deeper into the world of business, things quickly become more complicated.

Therefore, preparation and experience are keys to success in both business and chess. Shenk points out that Bobby Fisher supplemented his obvious aptitude for the game with thousands of hours of study. Well-known author Malcolm Gladwell writes about this essential combination of talent and preparation in his book *Outliers*. Ten thousand hours of practice, according to Gladwell, is what separates the Bobby Fishers of the world from other talented people who don't achieve the same success.

Similarly, in business, it is those leaders who know their discipline inside and out, and who spend years gaining knowledge and hard-won experience, who will best navigate the intricacies of their competitive environment. These leaders will win over the long haul.

One of history's famous chess players was Benjamin Franklin. He was an American founding father, diplomat, scientist, publisher and inventor. He was also a savvy businessman. Franklin said, "The Game of Chess is not merely an idle amusement. Several very valuable qualities of the mind, useful in the course of human life, are to be acquired or strengthened by it.... For life is a kind of Chess, in which we often have points to gain, and competitors or adversaries to deal with."

Franklin believed that chess sharpened his thinking, and that it taught several useful lessons. David Shenk explains that Franklin "asserted that the game improved a person's:

1) Foresight: looking ahead to the long-term consequences of any action.

2) Circumspection: surveying the entire scene, observing hidden dynamics and unseen possibilities.

3) Caution: avoiding haste and unnecessary blunders.

4) Perseverance: refusing to give up in dim circumstances, continually pushing to improve one's position."

There is one final way that business leaders can benefit from thinking like a chess player. Professor Dianne Horgan of Memphis State University has investigated how chess might improve various cognitive abilities. She found that, among other things, chess improves a person's self-perception.

Self-perception involves "calibration," which is the correlation between a person's perception of his or her own ability and the actual level of ability. In the population at large people generally have an overinflated view of their own talents. Improving calibration skills — by playing chess, for example — significantly enhances the value of feedback. If people have an accurate idea of their own level of competence, they are more open to input from others.

I would never advocate that every business leader should learn how to play chess in order to succeed in the world of "commercial activity." I would argue, however, that the thinking skills used by chess players are the same kind of skills that business leaders need to develop.

Business leaders need to work hard at learning their craft. They need knowledge, experience, and an in-depth technical understanding of their profession.

They also need to think strategically, which involves skills like considering long-term consequences, surveying the entire scene for all possible outcomes, proceeding with caution, and sticking to goals even when the going gets tough.

Finally, business leaders need to be receptive to feedback and to make adjustments as necessary to improve performance.

The leaders who display these qualities (whether they are actually chess players or not) stand the best chance of putting their competition into checkmate — and winning the game.

— CHAPTER ELEVEN —
DIVERSITY IS STRENGTH

"We all should know that diversity makes for a rich tapestry, and we must understand that all the threads of the tapestry are equal in value no matter what their color."

– Maya Angelou

From 1804 to 1806, U.S. Army officers Meriwether Lewis and William Clark led an amazing team known as the Corps of Discovery on an 8,000-mile journey over 863 days into the unknown reaches of the western United States, and then safely home again. They were commissioned by President Thomas Jefferson to find an all-water thoroughfare (the fabled Northwest Passage) to the Pacific Ocean. Though they failed in that mission (no such waterway existed on the route they would take) they succeeded in exploring and documenting virtually everything they saw along the way, establishing the boundaries of the young nation, and opening the great American West to future expansion.

What is perhaps most remarkable about Lewis and Clark and their incredible journey of discovery is that they achieved this feat, in a day and age when people gave no thought to the importance of incorporating and celebrating differences, with a team of talented individuals who were diverse in the broadest sense of the term. Lewis and Clark dramatically demonstrated a fundamental principle that all modern-day business leaders should know and understand: Diversity is strength.

We all remember the story from our school days of Sacagawea, the teenage Shoshone Indian woman who accompanied the expedition. She was the wife of Toussaint Charbonneau, who had been added to the team en route as an interpreter. Sacagawea was a nursing mother who traversed 5,000 miles with her infant son Jean Baptiste (known as "Pomp") on her back. There is a common misconception that she guided the expedition throughout the journey, which she did not, but her value to the Corps of Discovery was nevertheless profound. She was skilled and knowledgeable in field craft: building shelters, making and repairing clothing, and finding food. Through her quick thinking, she once saved valuable equipment and supplies when a canoe nearly capsized.

Most important, Sacagawea served as the physical embodiment of the Corps of Discovery's peaceful intentions. She was instrumental in securing necessary cooperation from Native American tribes along the way. Meriwether Lewis described Sacagawea as "our only dependence for a friendly negotiation with the Snake [Shoshone] Indians on whom we depend for horses to assist us in our portage from the Missouri to the Columbia River."

Another important member of the team was York, who was William Clark's black slave. In a time when it was a criminal offense for a slave to be taught how to operate a gun, York carried a musket throughout the expedition and used it with great skill to hunt. York was valuable during the many months spent rafting on a river because, unlike other members of the expedition, he could swim. York physically accompanied Clark on all of the most dangerous phases of the mission, suggesting that Clark fully trusted York's ability to handle any perilous situation. Finally, by virtue of his skin color, York fascinated the Indian tribes encountered on the journey. They referred to him as "Big Medicine." He was perceived as having greater value because of his uniqueness, and made negotiations with the Indians easier than they would otherwise have been. In the end, because of the special gifts they each brought, Sacagawea and York were regarded as essential and equal members of the team.

The Corps of Discovery was also diverse in less obvious ways. In an era when social status mattered a great deal, Lewis and Clark did not select a single member of the expedition based on any criteria other than merit. They cast their net far and wide in search of people who were not just physically strong, but who also possessed intelligence, discipline, and distinctive skills. One of the men they hired was a master carpenter, another was a veteran blacksmith. They recruited a tailor, a fisherman, a boatman, and several excellent hunters. They hired interpreters who would help them in their discussions with American Indian tribes. The team members came from a variety of cultures: Irish, German, French and English. There were several men who were mixed-race, half-white and half-Native American. All of the collective strengths and experiences the members of the Corps brought to the expedition combined effectively, even magically, to create a stronger team.

In his wonderful book, *Into the Unknown: Leadership Lessons From Lewis and Clark's Daring Westward Expedition*, author Jack Uldrich says, "It would be unrealistic to say that Lewis and Clark started their selection process with diversity as an end goal or even a deciding factor. As products of the late-eighteenth century, this was not how they thought. The lesson, however, is that by focusing on their end goal — reaching the Pacific — they were led, by necessity, to assemble a diverse team. As the famous architect Ludwig Mies van der Rohe said, 'Form follows function.' And to conquer the unknown, that 'form' manifested itself as a diverse team."

Even Lewis and Clark possessed complementary skills as co-commanders of the expedition. They were both seasoned soldiers, strong, and experienced in the ways of the wilderness. They were also curious, ambitious, and excellent leaders. But Lewis was better educated, and a superb hunter and botanist. Clark was a talented boatman and cartographer. Lewis tended to be reserved, humorless, and even prone to bouts of depression, while Clark was warm and engaging, with an easy manner that made him popular with his subordinates. Together they formed a formidable duo, arguably the most successful leadership team in American history.

Do you belong to a diverse business team? A team that is diverse not just in the obvious, visible sense, but that possesses diversity of skills, backgrounds, and experiences? Or does everyone on your team more or less think and act alike? With the increasing complexity of business missions in today's global economy, leaders who ignore the imperative to seek diversity in their approach will lose. As Lewis and Clark taught us so ably more than 200 years ago, diversity is an absolute necessity, because diversity is strength.

— CHAPTER TWELVE —
LEAD COURAGEOUSLY IN A CHALLENGING NEW WORLD

"The inexorable forces of competition and change catch up again with companies that restructure but do not revitalize, that cut people but do not fundamentally alter their ways of working."

– Sumantra Ghoshal

In 2001, at the beginning of a two-year recessionary period, Apple Computer experienced a revenue decline of 33 percent. Yet Apple bravely chose to increase research and development (R&D) expenditures by 13 percent, and continued to maintain that level of investment throughout the downward cycle. The innovative, groundbreaking technologies of the iTunes music store and software, the iPod Mini, and the iPod Photo were developed during this period. Apple experienced rapid and healthy growth.

Once again, in 2009, we are mired in a serious recession. Though there are signs that the economy is slowly improving, regardless of how the future takes shape, things will never be the same again. To quote the great philosopher Dorothy Gale from *The Wizard of Oz*, "We are not in Kansas anymore." Nevertheless those companies, such as Apple, that look to the future even when the current situation is precarious, will survive. For business leaders today, the critical new skill set is the ability to lead courageously in a challenging, unpredictable environment.

Survival in a deeply recessionary economy and building for a healthy future requires leaders to take on two important tasks. The first is to stabilize the business. The second involves adapting to a new and uncertain future and seizing opportunity wherever it presents itself.

The old adage "when you are up to your [posterior] in alligators, it's difficult to remember the original objective was to drain the pond," has come to my mind often during these trying times. The down economy has understandably caused businesses to focus attention on the immediate task of survival. Research shows that people are far more highly motivated to take action by the possibility of loss than by the prospect of gain.

Indeed, it makes sense during tough times to take every reasonable step to protect the existing business. Is your financial house in order? Are there opportunities to trim costs or otherwise gain efficiencies? Are you staffed and organized correctly? Does your product mix make sense? Is your product or service priced right? Are there opportunities to divest? These are all important questions that should already have been part of a rigorous review of your current business model.

The risk in undergoing this type of crisis-mode analysis involves the inclination to hunker down and wait out the storm once near-term steps are in place. All of us as leaders have a tendency to rely on skills and abilities that have worked for us in the past. We look for recognizable patterns so we can respond to them just as we have successfully done before. We want to be able to reassure our teams that things will return to normal soon. But there is great danger in this mind-set because the future that we face will be unlike anything any of us have ever previously experienced.

The businesses that will go beyond mere survival and thrive into the future are those that aggressively seize opportunity. They see lean times not as a disaster to endure, but as a challenge to overcome. During the recession of the early 2000s, approximately one in three industry leaders lost their perch at the top of their fields as savvy competitors maneuvered skillfully during the downturn. Those who follow bicycle racing know that in an event such as the Tour de France, the ultimate winner frequently overtakes the leaders during the mountain phase — the toughest part of the contest.

Do you have an opportunity to rethink your business model? In the recession of the early 1990s, IBM experienced its first revenue decline in more than fifty years. Losses mounted year after year. CEO Louis Gerstner took the opportunity during the downturn to seriously reconsider a business model based on sales of mainframe computers. IBM eventually shifted its focus from hardware to computer services and solutions, and it flourished.

Are you continuing to think about the future by investing in R&D, as Apple Computer did? Just as important, are you continuing to invest in your people? Remember, even during bad times, your top performers have other options. Do you have the right players in place? Are you encouraging them in their development? Do they see a future with your organization? I believe that one of the most short-sighted moves that many companies make when the going gets tough is to immediately cut training and development dollars.

Finally, these pragmatic steps of rethinking your business model, investing in R&D, and taking care of your people should not just be one-time responses to a crisis, but rather an ongoing part of how you do business. In a *Harvard Business Review* article from 2003, business authors Gary Hamel and Liisa Valikangas state that the strongest businesses are those that continuously "reinvent business models and strategies as circumstances change," rather than just making singular adjustments in reaction to an emergency. The authors argue that those companies that work incrementally to try numerous different ideas on a micro scale — while involving many people in the discovery process — succeed over time. Businesses "should steer clear of grand, imperial strategies and devote themselves instead to launching a swarm of low-risk experiments."

No matter how we cut it, the future is daunting and unknowable. But it is also rich with abundant opportunity. Leaders who work hard to strengthen their organizations in the short run, and then courageously look to the future, will end up on top of the mountain when the economy improves. A continuous cycle of scrutinizing the business model, investing in lots of new ideas, and developing people will bring success in a challenging new world.

– CHAPTER THIRTEEN –
CORPORATE SOCIAL RESPONSIBILITY IS GOOD BUSINESS STRATEGY

*"The manager does things right; the
leader does the right thing."*

– Warren Bennis

Lou Miller has owned and operated Big Apple Bagels in Apple Valley, Minnesota, for the past eleven years. At the end of each day, she donates whatever bagels she has left over to a variety of non-profits, such as food shelves, veterans groups, and schools. Lou can't say for sure whether the donations have significantly improved her bottom line, but she does know that this small gesture of giving away excess food on a daily basis has generated goodwill for her business. Most important to Lou, it just feels like the right thing to do.

Some business leaders believe that their only obligation is to their shareholders. These managers assert that the sole objective in business is to improve profitability for the benefit of the owners of the firm. However, American consumers are beginning to strongly reward businesses that see their mission more broadly. Many companies, big and small, are becoming aware of (and acting upon) an important economic reality: Corporate social responsibility is good business strategy.

Corporate social responsibility (CSR) involves an array of steps that a company can take to contribute back to the community: philanthropy, product donations, volunteerism, cause-marketing (for example, providing business expertise to nonprofit groups), and citizenship, especially around environmental sustainability. While it is no doubt more difficult to precisely measure return on investment for these types of activities, abundant data demonstrate the economic benefits of CSR. DePaul University conducted a study in 2002 that compared the performance of the 100 Best Corporate Citizens from *Business Ethics* magazine against the remainder of the S&P 500. In measurements such as sales growth, profit, and return on equity, the socially responsible companies exceeded the competition by 10 percent.

A *Time* magazine article from September 2009, entitled "The Responsibility Revolution," cites a 2007 Goldman Sachs report that concluded that companies with a focus on sustainability outperformed the overall market, frequently by a significant margin. PricewaterhouseCoopers recently completed a study that showed a better return on assets for companies that reported sustainability information over those firms that did not share such data.

Time conducted a poll which showed that more than 60 percent of Americans have purchased organic products since January 2009.

Almost 40 percent say that they bought products this year because of the social or political values of the company that sold the merchandise. *Time* says, "What we are discovering now, in the most uncertain economy since [the Great Depression], is that enlightened self-interest — call it a shared sense of responsibility — is good economics.... We are starting to put our money where our ideals are."

Many organizations have long understood the importance of CSR. More than thirty years ago, twenty-three Minnesota companies formed the Keystone Program. Participating firms each contribute at least 2 percent of annual pretax earnings back into their communities. Today, there are more than 200 members of Keystone.

Target Corporation (a charter Keystone member as Dayton Hudson) contributes 5 percent of pre-tax earnings, in good times and in bad. I recently spoke with my friend and former colleague Gail Dorn, who was for many years the Vice President of Communications and Community Relations at Target.

Gail talked about Target's enduring culture and tradition of giving back, and she indicated there were many times when it would have been easy to cut the program. She recalled, "Analysts would challenge us, asking why we were giving away 5 percent? [Target leadership] ignored their pleas. Even though a return on investment was difficult to measure, Target's community programs generated incredible goodwill. Our customers loved that we always took the extra step to become integrated in the community. This was particularly helpful in 1987 when Dayton Hudson sought public support to fend off a hostile takeover attempt."

Another mighty Minnesota corporation that appreciates the importance of CSR is the Best Buy Company. An article in the December 7, 2009 issue of *Fortune* magazine describes Best Buy's free recycling program. Since March, when Best Buy began offering free recycling of TVs, computers and any other electronic gadgets, more than 25 million pounds of old devices have been turned in at Best Buy's 1,004 U.S. store locations. *Fortune* says, "The company's massive recycling program seems expensive to run, until you look at all the benefits: a green reputation, a focus on service, and a fresh way to get customers into the stores. No wonder Best Buy has learned to love old TVs and eight-track tape players."

Best Buy's leadership understands that the take-back program will probably be, at best, a break-even proposition. Nevertheless, profit and loss consequences aside, Best Buy CEO Brian Dunn described how he feels when a customer drops off an old TV set: "I'm happy because it helps make the connection between Best Buy and the customer and the community."

Sometimes, financial outcomes are not the most important consideration in business.

Small and medium-size companies should take heed of the responsibility revolution as well. *Time* points out that many shoppers consider not only the nature of the product they buy, but where it came from. More than 80 percent of consumers say they have deliberately supported local and neighborhood businesses (like Big Apple Bagels) that demonstrate a corporate conscience and concern for the environment. Also, there are more than 250 socially responsible investment mutual funds (consisting generally of companies that do not profit from tobacco, oil or child labor) that today manage approximately $2.7 trillion in wealth.

Time concludes, "… Americans are recalibrating our sense of what it means to be a citizen, not just through voting or volunteering, but also through commerce: by what we buy…. That's evidence of a changing mind-set, a new kind of social contract among consumers, business, and government. We are seeing the rise of the citizen consumer — and the beginning of a responsibility revolution." Indeed, smart companies today have seen the future and are taking action. These companies know that corporate social responsibility is good business strategy.

– CHAPTER FOURTEEN –
MOTIVATE YOUR PEOPLE

"The common wisdom is that…. managers have to learn to motivate people. Nonsense. Employees bring their own motivation."

– Tom Peters

A colleague recently told me that his supervisor had recognized and rewarded his job performance in two ways in the past year. First, he had extended an extremely large salary increase. Next, at year-end, he sent a bottle of wine and a handwritten note, expressing his appreciation for all that my friend had accomplished professionally during the year. For this employee, when I asked which gesture meant the most to him, the wine and the note were far and away more significant than the salary adjustment. His boss took the time in a thoughtful, personal, and unforgettable way to call out his outstanding work. This outcome may seem counterintuitive to many leaders because, unfortunately, many leaders have a misconception about what motivates their people.

In her book, *An Honest Day's Work*, author Twyla Dell writes, "The heart of motivation is to give people what they really want most from work. The more you are able to provide what they want, the more you should expect what you really want, namely: productivity, quality, and service." How do managers face the understandable difficulty in giving people "what they want" when individual employees are motivated in different ways and by different things? While adequate pay matters — most people are unwilling to work for nothing — it is a mistake to assume that economic gain is the only factor that motivates people to do good work.

Indeed, a significant body of research indicates that what motivates people to do high-quality work revolves much more directly around intrinsic factors, rather than rewards or punishment. Those companies that build a culture in which motivation just naturally happens will outperform those that still rely on an outmoded "carrot-and-stick" approach.

In his seminal 2003 book, *The Motivation to Work*, scholar Frederick Herzberg (along with co-authors Bernard Mausner and Barbara Bloch Snyderman) makes the simple but compelling point that human beings are motivated from within, not by any policy imposed by their company. Herzberg significantly influenced human resource management by conducting an extensive series of interviews that explored employee attitudes and attempted to get at the question "What motivates employees?"

Herzberg identifies two critical sets of factors that influence motivation. The first set, which he calls hygiene factors, includes basic needs such as working conditions, benefits, job security and company policies. Poor hygiene factors can lead to employee dissatisfaction. Improvement in hygiene factors represents a step in the right direction, but will not in itself inspire motivation.

The second set, called motivation factors, go beyond fundamental working conditions and to the heart of what energizes people: a sense of achievement, opportunities to develop, and recognition, all of which lead to improved job satisfaction. Ultimately, argues Herzberg, companies succeed by motivating people through job enrichment rather than reward or pressure.

In his recent bestseller, *Drive: The Surprising Truth About What Motivates Us*, author Dan Pink describes his own list of the key factors that motivate people: autonomy, mastery, and purpose. Pink says, "The baseline rewards must be sufficient. That is, the team's basic compensation must be adequate and fair.... Your [organization] must be a congenial place to work. And the people on your team must have autonomy, they must have ample opportunity to pursue mastery, and their daily routines must relate to a higher purpose. If these elements are in place, the best strategy is to provide a sense of urgency and significance — and then get out of the talent's way."

During World War II, the Lockheed Aircraft Corporation established what became the first "skunk works" (a project team that is provided great autonomy to work on high priority tasks), to develop the first U.S. jet fighter. The experiment was a great success. The team of 53 engineers and support staff worked in secrecy in a remote location. The culture was characterized by equal treatment, informality, limited bureaucracy, and open and honest exchange of ideas. Leadership guru Warren Bennis describes the lead designer on the project as "a visionary on at least two fronts: designing airplanes and organizing genius. [He] seemed to know intuitively what talented people needed to do their best work, how to motivate them, and how to make sure the desired product was created as quickly and cheaply as possible."

What can your organization do to create an environment in which motivation is the natural outcome of a healthy culture and not a matter of following a rewards-and-punishment dynamic?

- Ask people what they want. Talk to your folks and listen to what they tell you. Find out what motivates each individual on your team and (within reason) work to meet those needs. Treat people with respect.

- Make sure that your people are paid fairly, especially in comparison to those who are doing similar work in other organizations. If working conditions are not up to an acceptable standard, fix them.

- Encourage an open and vigorous exchange of ideas. Evaluate mistakes honestly to learn from them, without assigning blame.

- If you are considering financial or other extrinsic rewards, know that research indicates (as author Dan Pink reminds us) "Any extrinsic reward should be unexpected and offered only after the task is complete. Holding out a prize at the beginning of a project — and offering it as a contingency — will inevitably focus people's attention on obtaining the reward rather than attacking the problem."

- Appreciate the power of a small gesture of gratitude, such as a handwritten note or a pat on the back. Sometimes the simplest recognition, as long as it's timely, specific and sincere, can have a hugely motivating effect (just ask my friend about the note he received from his boss).

Human beings are complicated, and each of us experiences motivation differently. But we all have a basic and inherent need to feel that we have control of our lives, that we are learning and growing, and that our work has a larger meaning beyond a mere paycheck. Organizations that recognize these fundamental truths will do well on the shoulders of a highly motivated workforce.

– CHAPTER FIFTEEN –
CELEBRATE ENTREPRENEURSHIP

"Entrepreneurs have no frontier other than their own ambition."

– Robert Heller

I had the opportunity to work at Best Buy from 2001 to 2009. Although the company was formed in 1966 — almost 45 years ago — I was always surprised and impressed to see the founder, Richard Schulze, as a frequent presence at corporate headquarters. While Dick Schulze long ago turned over day-to-day operational responsibility and decision making to others, his innovative spirit, willingness to take risks, and drive for results are still very much a part of the corporate culture. Even thought Best Buy is now one of the largest business enterprises in America with almost $50 billion in revenues and 150,000 employees, it is still a company that celebrates entrepreneurship.

It is absolutely fascinating to contemplate that every business in the world started as nothing more than an idea in someone's head. Examples of huge enterprises that began with the innovation of a single founder include General Electric (Thomas Edison), Walmart (Sam Walton), Toyota Motor (Kiichiro Toyoda), and Mary Kay Inc. (Mary Kay Ash). Each of these entrepreneurs either had a new and better idea, or got sick of working for someone else, or both. And he or she also invariably had a high tolerance for uncertainty and an intense determination to succeed.

It is this powerful spirit of entrepreneurship without which we could not survive and the world economy would crumble. While clearly not everyone is cut out to be an entrepreneur, we all desperately need and depend on these founding visionaries (whatever the size of the enterprise they invent) to continue to innovate, to strive, and to build.

Are entrepreneurs born, or can they be made? There is a strong difference of opinion as to whether or not entrepreneurship can be taught. If the increase in formal entrepreneurial education over the last thirty-plus years is any indication, many business schools believe that entrepreneurial skills can be learned. Today, better than 2,000 American colleges and universities offer classes in entrepreneurship, compared to a paltry 200 back in the 1970s.

Gregg Fairbrothers is the founding director of the Dartmouth Entrepreneurial Network, and he teaches a hugely successful course in entrepreneurship at the Tuck School of Business. In Fairbrothers's class the students learn through experience; the vast majority of the work takes place outside the classroom. Students develop and present their own ideas for a startup, and then are tasked with refining their approach, testing in the marketplace, and pitching to potential investors to secure financing. Clearly, Fairbrothers believes that learning by doing in the hard school of the marketplace is the only way to teach entrepreneurship.

Fairbrothers also acknowledges that entrepreneurship is a difficult concept to define and measure with any precision. He suggests that entrepreneurs are characterized more by a set of identifiable traits than by what they do, and that the range of entrepreneurial behaviors can be plotted along a classic bell curve. In a recent *Fortune* magazine article Fairbrothers says, "So the question is, can you take a point on that curve and move it? If 'entrepreneurial' is to the right, can you move it that way? I know I can move it that way. I've done it."

Entrepreneurship, therefore, is not a single trait that some individuals and organizations possess and others do not. It is not an all-or-nothing proposition, but rather a spectrum of behaviors that includes innovative approaches, calculated risks, and willingness to fail and try again.

Starbucks CEO Howard Schultz recently held a series of brainstorming meetings with a group of his employees. Schultz was the entrepreneurial visionary behind the massive growth of the Starbucks brand. He left the company for a time only to return in 2008 as Starbucks struggled to maintain its impressive growth. The employee focus group helped in the effort to return to entrepreneurial roots. Schultz says in a recent *New York Times* interview, "We lost our way... [so] we went back to start-up mode, hand-to-hand combat every day. And with the kind of discussion and focus that probably we had not had as a company since the early days: the fear of failure, the hunger to win."

Among other things, Starbucks now works to give its stores a local feel that reflects neighborhood history and architecture, and even displays the work of local artists. The company places greater emphasis on satisfying regional differences among coffee drinkers; Sun Belt customers prefer cold drinks and those in the Pacific Northwest drink more espresso, for example. Starbucks coffee buyers no longer focus exclusively on purchasing only beans produced in sufficient quantity to supply all stores; they now also buy local blends made in small batches.

Although the jury is still out, as of early 2010, Starbucks had seen healthy increases in revenues, same-store sales, and its stock price. Leadership expert Warren Bennis says of entrepreneurs such as Schulz that they "keep shaking things up and pulling the stakes out of the tent because they like the mud and the chaos of reinventing, and Howard has a bit of that in him."

Do you as a leader display entrepreneurial behaviors? Do you like to shake things up, try new ideas, and take the occasional calculated risk? How about the organization you work for? Where does it sit on the "entrepreneurial bell curve"? Do you celebrate entrepreneurship or have you become bureaucratic and stagnant? No matter the age or size of your enterprise (think of Best Buy Co.), a conscious effort to cultivate and maintain entrepreneurial roots can provide a healthy boost in performance.

– CHAPTER SIXTEEN –
EMPOWER AND ENGAGE WOMEN

"Too seldom does the world pause to consider how much kinder and more humane business has become since women invaded the marketplace."

– Edith Johnson

There is a Chinese proverb that says, "Women hold up half the sky." The great American novelist and humorist Mark Twain once asked rhetorically, "What would men be without women?" His answer: "Scarce, sir, mighty scarce."

Women have made huge strides in recent decades in the long and challenging quest for equality. In the United States, we see many more women in positions of power in government and business. Hillary Rodham Clinton narrowly missed in her recent bid for the presidency, but we still fall woefully short of the mark.

Today, smart businesses work incredibly hard to develop and retain their female employees and to listen and market to their female customers. The leaders who run these businesses know that the best and highest functioning of both our national and world economies will never come to pass until the day when women become fully empowered and engaged.

It is difficult to imagine that less than a hundred years ago women were not even allowed to vote in the United States. Since then, we have undeniably made enormous progress. Yet while women make up more than half of our labor force, as of mid-2009 only fifteen Fortune 500 companies (3 percent) had female CEOs. In Minnesota, only six of the state's top 100 public companies have female CEOs, and women hold only 15 percent of the executive officer positions in those 100 leading companies. The situation is far worse in other parts of the world.

In their powerful and heart-rending book *Half the Sky: Turning Oppression Into Opportunity For Women Worldwide*, the Pulitzer Prize-winning husband-and-wife team of Nicholas Kristof and Sheryl WuDunn describe what they characterize as the greatest human rights violation of our time: the oppression of women and girls in the developing world. The authors tell stories about three particularly horrific abuses: sex trafficking and forced prostitution; gender-based violence, such as honor killings and mass rape; and maternal mortality, which claims one woman per minute in the developing world.

Their message, however, is not one of despair but of hope. They write, "Many of the stories in this book are wrenching, but keep in mind this central truth: Women aren't the problem but the solution. The plight of girls is no more tragedy than an opportunity."

Kristof and WuDunn suggest that the answer to the problem lies in educating women and fully incorporating them into the economic life of their communities and countries. They describe the dramatic results in East Asia of what they call the "girl effect," saying, "Women are indeed a linchpin of the region's development strategy.... These countries took young women who previously had contributed negligibly to gross national product and injected them into the economy, hugely increasing the labor force. The basic formula was to ease repression, educate girls as well as boys, give the girls the freedom to move to cities and take factory jobs, and then benefit from a demographic dividend as they delayed marriage and reduced childbearing. The women meanwhile... saved enough of their pay to boost national savings rates.... Evidence has mounted that helping women can be a successful poverty-fighting strategy anywhere in the world, not just in the booming economies of East Asia."

Indeed, the data is insurmountable that fully including women in the workplace — especially in positions of leadership — results in superior economic outcomes. One study found that the one quarter of American Fortune 500 companies with the most female executives had a 35 percent better return on equity than the one quarter of companies with the fewest. Studies show that female executives generally tend to avoid unnecessary risk and focus patiently on the long term, while also bringing a more collaborative, conciliatory, and motivational leadership style, which is well-suited to today's less hierarchical workplace. Women will play an increasingly important future role, because in an era when new jobs will demand better educated workers, women now receive the majority of college and advanced degrees.

Women are a force to be reckoned with as customers as well. Companies that sell products as varied as consumer electronics, health care, and cars overlook women at their peril, because the woman of the house controls an astounding 83 percent of all consumer purchases.

Insightful and forward-looking companies focus on their female customers and also create positive work environments for their female workers, many of whom are striving mightily to balance professional and family obligations. These companies emphasize business outcomes rather than long hours in the office. At Best Buy, a program called ROWE (results-only work environment) improved productivity in some departments by as much as 40 percent. In 2009, NetApp improved market share, avoided layoffs, and accumulated $2 billion in cash reserves, while still offering employees paid time off for volunteer work, adoption aid, and autism coverage. The biotech company Genentech, saw revenues jump by 25 percent early last year, while featuring on-site daycare, a fitness center, and paid sabbaticals. Examples such as these are legion, and the economic case is undeniable.

Where does your organization, company, or team sit with respect to women? Do women possess a truly participatory voice, or are they underrepresented and marginalized? Are there women in leadership roles in your organization? Do you recognize the power of women as consumers of your products or services? Do you thoughtfully cultivate them as customers? If you answer no to these questions, then perhaps now is the time to do your part to make changes in your organization that will help bring us to the day when the feminine half of all who must together hold up the sky will be fully empowered and engaged.

– PART THREE –
COMMUNICATION

*"The single biggest problem in communication
is the illusion that it has taken place."*

– George Bernard Shaw

– CHAPTER SEVENTEEN –
APPRECIATE THE POWER OF WORDS

"... that we here highly resolve that these dead shall not have died in vain, that this nation under God shall have a new birth of freedom, and that government of the people, by the people, for the people shall not perish from the earth."

– Abraham Lincoln

As business leaders we often fail to fully appreciate the ability we possess, for both good and ill, to influence people and situations through the simple choice of the words we use. Our teams are listening closely to what we say. The very best communicators select their words carefully and work hard to ensure that followers understand their meaning. This necessity to speak and write clearly is a basic leadership objective, but ever so difficult to consistently execute.

Recently, I was honored to take a group of executives through a leadership seminar at the Gettysburg battlefield in Pennsylvania. At the end of our day-long tour of that sacred place, one of the participants read Abraham Lincoln's Gettysburg Address near the spot where Lincoln delivered it at the National Cemetery in November 1863. As she read that beautiful little speech (only 272 words long),

I was reminded of the power of an idea well-expressed to move people to think differently and, sometimes, to change the world.

Lincoln had less than a year of formal schooling but he read constantly from an early age in an effort to educate himself. He became a master communicator whose innate yet carefully honed abilities as a story-teller and humorist enabled him to reach and teach ordinary people in unforgettable fashion. His deep study of the *Holy Bible* and Shakespeare influenced the lovely cadences of his speeches.

Lincoln's masterpiece, the Gettysburg Address, forever changed the way Americans think of themselves. In the speech, he explained the meaning of the sacrifice of so many lives on the battlefield just a few months prior. He asserted the Declaration of Independence and its central idea- equality- as a matter of founding law. The Civil War, Lincoln told us, was the great struggle around and testing of this new principle. As historian Gary Wills said, "By accepting the Gettysburg Address, its concept of a single people dedicated to a proposition, we have been changed. Because of it, we live in a different America."

Few people, even among great historical figures, have Abraham Lincoln's gift for language. Of speeches that compare with the Gettysburg Address, for me, only the inspirational words of Dr. Martin Luther King Jr. come to mind, delivered on the steps of the Lincoln Memorial in August 1963, telling his countrymen: "I have a dream today…."

So what does that leave for those of us who are mere mortals? For those of us who often get tangled in our own syntax? For those of us who dread having to put our thoughts down on paper?

There is a popular historical myth that Lincoln penned the Gettysburg Address on the back of an envelope as he rode the train from Washington, D.C., to Pennsylvania. To the contrary, the speech was carefully composed beforehand at the White House. He wrote and rewrote, revising the speech even as late as the morning of the day it was to be delivered. Lincoln was incredibly particular in his choice of words, and he worked hard to get the message just right. He knew that his followers, and even future generations, would be paying close attention. In that way, he was a teacher to all of us who would aspire to be leaders who communicate well.

With written communication, take the time to be thoughtful. Who is your intended audience? What message do you want to convey? How can you write that piece — whether a short e-mail or a full-blown speech — in the simplest, most concise way, yet still get your point across (remember Lincoln's 272 words)?

Nothing is more frustrating for a team of people than to read something their boss or colleague has produced that causes confusion. Credibility is lost and time is wasted. Proofread what you write. Better yet, have someone whom you trust check your work. Be open to suggestions and make changes accordingly. Like Lincoln did, practice your writing. As with any other skill, writing ability can be developed over time with effort, repetition, and feedback.

The spoken word can prove more difficult because we frequently don't have time to be as reflective as we might with a writing assignment. We are often called upon to give an opinion quickly without the benefit of all the information we need to make a judgment. Still, the best communicators are thoughtful in speech as well.

Take a moment before you speak. Collect your thoughts. Consider the audience. It's okay to acknowledge what you don't know and take time to do some research. Gather data. Ask good questions. Select your words. Deliver them well. Confirm understanding.

As always, the old saying holds true: "Talk is cheap, but whiskey costs money." Words without appropriate and consistent actions to back them up are only words. With that said, leadership begins with words. Especially in the difficult economic environment in which we all live and work, anxious business teams are keenly in tune with what leadership is saying. So take the opportunity to be thoughtful with your words. The future of your organization may depend on it.

— CHAPTER EIGHTEEN —
COMMUNICATE, COMMUNICATE, COMMUNICATE

"If I had a brick for every time I've repeated the phrase 'Quality, Service, Cleanliness and Value,' I'd probably be able to bridge the Atlantic Ocean with them."

— Ray Kroc

Drew Gilpin Faust is a noted American historian who specializes in the history of the South and, in particular, the changing roles of women during the period before and during the Civil War. She taught for many years at the University of Pennsylvania and is the award-winning author of several books. In 2001 she became the head of the Radcliffe Institute for Advanced Study and in 2007 she was named the first female president of Harvard University.

In a recent interview in the *New York Times*, Gilpin Faust describes the leadership lessons she learned in making the transition from her role as a scholar to that of an administrator with responsibility for a team of people and a large, complex organization. She says, "They have to do with understanding the context in which you are leading. Universities have enormously distributed authority and many different sorts of constituencies, all of whom have a stake in that institution.... I spend a huge amount of time reaching out to people, either literally or digitally, and with alumni networks all over the world, so that I can connect. Leadership by walking around — that's a digital space now, it's virtual space."

Good communication is the key to effective performance, innovation, and change in any organization. And the message must be hammered home repeatedly. Gilpin Faust says, "When I came to the Radcliffe Institute for Advanced Study, many people wanted to help. An alum who was an expert in turnarounds said, 'One lesson about change in any organization: communicate, communicate, communicate.'"

Susan Docherty, who heads up the United States sales, service, and marketing team at General Motors, echoes Gilpin Faust's point of view concerning uniformity and persistence in communication. Docherty says in a recent interview, "Whether you have a really small team or a really big team, communication needs to be at the forefront. It needs to be simple. It needs to be consistent. And even when you're tired of what the message is, you need to do it again and again and again, because everybody comes to the table with a different perspective and a different experience. The same words mean different things to different people."

The global consulting firm Watson Wyatt reports in a survey just released for 2009-10 that companies that communicate effectively provided a 47 percent higher return to their shareholders over the five-year period from 2004 to 2009. The report states, "In challenging times, companies are forced to make tough decisions and deliver difficult messages. But our study found that high-performing companies don't shy away from tough messages. They make communication a priority and use every tool available to reach out to a workforce in desperate need of information and direction."

Specifically, the Watson Wyatt study reveals that the companies that communicate best are very courageous in their employee communication. Watson Wyatt refers to this skill as "telling it like it is." Instead of shying away from difficult messages in an attempt to protect their people, these companies train and encourage their managers to focus on constant, effective communication, especially during times of uncertainty. "Highly effective communicators," says Watson Wyatt, "say more, not less." The study shows that when people are told what they need to know, even if the news is bad, their performance actually improves.

The best companies also promote innovation through their communication plans by encouraging employees to think creatively about work processes, job tasks, and productivity measures. Even the communication plans themselves reflect an innovative spirit. They use multiple channels such as intranet updates, wikis, blogs, and e-mail, as well as face-to-face dialogue where possible. The report asserts, "... taking the initiative to try new tools to reach a culturally diverse and geographically dispersed audience is the hallmark of effective communication." This is the essence of "leadership by walking around in a virtual space" that Drew Gilpin Faust describes.

The highest-performing companies are disciplined in their approach to communication. They set direction and measure results to ensure that employees know what they are supposed to be doing and why. They make sure that employees are given good direction within a helpful context. The result is a more engaged team. Outcomes, both good and bad, are measured closely and shared with the team.

Finally, the Watson Wyatt report emphasizes that a critical component of any solid communication plan involves listening to employees. Good communication ensures alignment, but if companies are not confirming understanding and listening to feedback, then alignment can be compromised.

Clearly, those organizations — whether they are a major university or a small business — that develop simple, consistent messages and repeat them constantly through multiple channels perform best over time. Gilpin Faust sums up the point well when she talks about her most critical lesson in communication: "Someone would say, 'Well, you've never talked about X,' and I'd say, 'I've talked about it here, here, and here. I talk about that all the time. Then I realize that all the time isn't enough. You have to do 'all the time and more.'"

In other words, communicate, communicate, communicate.

– CHAPTER NINETEEN –
SEEK AND PROVIDE HONEST FEEDBACK

"No organizational action has more power for motivating employee behavior change than feedback from credible work associates."

– Mark R. Edwards

Robert Gates is America's secretary of defense. He has served six presidential administrations, starting as a staffer at the National Security Council during the presidency of Gerald Ford. Gates became a CIA expert on the Soviet Union under Jimmy Carter, deputy director of the CIA for Ronald Reagan, and CIA director for the first President Bush. The second President Bush named Gates secretary of defense in 2006. With the election of Barack Obama, Gates became the only defense secretary ever asked to continue to serve a new administration of a rival party. Gates survives and thrives out of intelligence, determination, adaptability, and pragmatism. He also succeeds in significant part from his willingness, without fail, to seek and provide honest feedback.

Gates is clear in communicating priorities and providing straightforward feedback to his people. When he is disappointed in his team's performance, he takes swift action. In 2006, word leaked out that there were miserable conditions at the Walter Reed Army Medical Center, and a cumbersome bureaucracy prevented wounded soldiers from receiving necessary medical care. Gates fired not only the hospital commander but the secretary and the surgeon general of the army as well. In 2010, when defense contractor Lockheed Martin's F-35 stealth-fighter-jet program was plagued by technical problems and cost overruns, Gates dismissed the military officer who managed the program and withheld more than $600 million in fees from Lockheed Martin. The message in both cases was clear: We will take care of our soldiers, and military programs will come in on time and within budget under Secretary Gates.

But Gates is a leader who not only provides unambiguous direction to his team; he also seeks feedback in return. Gates has formed a solid partnership with Secretary of State Hillary Clinton, and she explains the success of that critical political relationship by saying simply, "He listens more than he talks."

In a recent interview in a national news publication, a journalist asked Gates several questions about whether he was a man of vision or merely a competent functionary who understands how to navigate Washington's complexity. In an extraordinary exchange, when one of his aides felt that Gates was waffling in his answers, the aide — not the interviewer — intervened aggressively and pushed Gates to clarify his point of view. Instead of becoming angry, Gates's reaction was to calmly contemplate the question more deeply and come up with a better response. When asked about the key to good leadership Gates says, "Offer candor, encourage candor, stand up for what you think is right. Don't be buffaloed, because generals — and secretaries — can be wrong." Clearly, the men and women serving under Robert Gates feel comfortable in giving him brutally honest input, and he listens to and incorporates their feedback.

Good business leaders also demonstrate skill at giving and receiving feedback. Omar Hamoui is the founder and CEO of AdMob, a mobile advertising network. Hamoui described AdMob's cultural propensity for honest conversations in a recent interview: "Nobody at AdMob is shy to point out a problem or an issue with a product or service, even if it's a product or service that they didn't build or they don't own…. We're just very, very upfront about those things."

And how does Hamoui also ensure that he is receiving the feedback he needs to hear? In addition to 360 reviews from his team, he says, "A lot of it is informal. If you make yourself available to people, they'll tell you what they think. I don't have an office. We have an open office here. I also move my desk around. About every six weeks or so I just move to another part of the company that I feel I haven't heard a lot about lately or don't know the people that well in, and I just sort of sit there…. if people see you just sitting there and you're not doing anything, they walk up to you and talk to you."

Savvy business managers seek feedback not only from their employees, but they also want to know what their customers have to say. The March 2010 issue of *Fast Company* magazine features the efforts of the restaurant chain Houlihan's to court information from its customers. In the summer of 2009, Houlihan's created its own social networking site, called HQ. The "formerly stodgy Irish pub" invited 10,500 select customers to become "Houlifans," with a mission of providing feedback that allows the chain to revamp menus and service quickly. The main benefit comes in that each individual restaurant averages 200 to 400 Houlifans, who consistently bring friends with them when they come in to dine. Overall profits went up 12% in the Kansas City area, site of the first pilot program. All thanks to a willingness to hear feedback, whether good, bad, or indifferent.

In a famous story from Abraham Lincoln's presidency, Secretary of War Edwin Stanton once called Lincoln a "damn fool" for signing an executive order with which Stanton disagreed. Word got back to Lincoln of Stanton's statement. Instead of becoming indignant or defensive, Lincoln said, "If Stanton said I am a damned fool, then I must be, for he is nearly always right. I'll just step over and see for myself." Lincoln met with Stanton, listened carefully to his concerns, and became convinced to withdraw the order.

How brave and diligent are you as a business leader in seeking and providing honest feedback? Does the culture of your team or organization encourage honest input from employees and customers? Do you respond to feedback in a composed and rational way that allows necessary change to take place? The best leaders from history and right up to the present day are adept at both telling and hearing the truth.

– CHAPTER TWENTY –
TAKE TIME TO CONCENTRATE

"Intense concentration for hour after hour can bring out resources in people that they didn't know they had."

– Edwin Land

Way back in the old days (early 1990s), when I worked for the Target Corporation, I used to exercise over the noon hour at the Northwest Arena Club in downtown Minneapolis. I remember watching with great amusement as a stressed-out attorney whom I knew would run countless laps around the indoor track while dictating into a hand-held recording device. I imagined his executive assistant struggling to transcribe his breathless memos. He was truly the Neanderthal version of today's "multitasker."

A recent *New York Times* front page story is entitled, "Hooked on Gadgets, and Paying a Mental Price: Constant Use Takes a Toll on Concentration and Family Life." The article highlights the challenges faced by Kord Campbell, founder of an Internet start-up company. Campbell is so addicted to e-mail and the Internet that, "Even after he unplugs, he craves the stimulation he gets from his electronic gadgets. He forgets things like dinner plans, and he has trouble focusing on his family. His wife, Brenda, complains, 'It seems like he can no longer be fully in the moment.'"

Kord Campbell's saga — cautionary tale though it may be — probably sounds familiar to most of us. Perhaps it's even uncomfortably familiar. How much time do you spend sifting through and responding to e-mail on a daily basis? How much time surfing the Web? How much do you love video games? Are you at a loss without your laptop, iPhone, or Blackberry? When was the last time you spent several hours, uninterrupted by devices, working on a critical issue or problem?

In this age of astounding technical wizardry, smart business people still recognize that excessive devotion to our electronic lifelines can be a distraction and siphon time from important matters. Though our ability to communicate has been vastly enhanced in recent times, our ability to focus has not. Awareness of this conundrum is essential to enabling us to step back and carry out a very important leadership responsibility: taking time to concentrate.

Entrepreneur magazine published a piece in March 2010 called, "E-mail Is Making You Stupid." Business reporter Joe Robinson tells us that the average office worker checks e-mail 50 times and sends 77 instant messages daily. The typical employee loses more than two hours per day in productivity as a result of electronic interruptions. Computer chip maker Intel generated an estimate of how much money large companies lose annually from distractions caused by excessive e-mails, and the answer was $2 billion. The situation is not getting better. The E-Policy Institute warns that e-mail volume is growing by a rate of 66% per year. This electronic deluge not only costs companies dearly in productivity, it creates incredible stress, decreases job satisfaction, and diminishes creativity.

In his book, *The Shallows: What the Internet Is Doing to Our Brains*, technology author Nicholas Carr argues that the very way we think and experience the world has been dramatically altered by the Internet. Studies demonstrate that extended use of the Internet quickly and significantly alters the brain's neural pathways, creating a tendency to skim rather than read closely, become easily distracted, and learn only superficially. Research also demonstrates that people who read linear text (as in a book) comprehend and remember more than those who read text with numerous links, as on the Internet. Carr says, "Once I was a scuba diver in a sea of words. Now I zip along the surface like a guy on a Jet Ski."

Some people claim to be able to manage myriad electronic inputs and remain highly productive because they are "multitaskers." Unfortunately, their imagined ability is a myth. Joe Robinson says, "The cult of multitasking would have us believe that compulsive message checking is the behavior of an always-on, hyper-productive worker. But it's not. It's the sign of a distracted employee who misguidedly believes he can do multiple tasks at one time. Science disagrees. People may be able to chew gum and walk at the same time, but they can't do two or more thinking tasks simultaneously."

Critics point to studies that suggest that some cognitive tasks, like visual perception and sustained attention, actually improve as a result of using screen-based technologies. Many scientists, however, suggest that more brain activity is not necessarily better brain activity. Developmental psychologist Patricia Greenfield asserts, "Every medium develops some cognitive skills at the expense of others." She acknowledges that use of the Web has led to the "widespread development of visual-spatial skills," but simultaneously we have lost "deep processing" capabilities that are foundational to "mindful knowledge acquisition, inductive analysis, critical thinking, imagination, and reflection."

Some companies understand the new reality and are fighting back. Intel has implemented "Quiet Time" at two of its locations. During designated Quiet Time, no one is allowed to engage in messaging or phone contact. Employees are expected to concentrate and work quietly on an individual basis. Companies such as Deloitte & Touche and U.S. Cellular have mandated restricted e-mail use and encouraged face-to-face meetings. They have also tried such ideas as "no e-mail Friday."

What can individuals do to carve out time to concentrate and get work done?

- Check e-mail only a few times daily, rather than continuously, and let people know that you will check messages at 8 a.m., noon, and 4 p.m.
- Whenever possible, meet face-to-face or talk by phone as the preferred mode of communication.
- Prioritize your tasks for the day, and set aside time to focus quietly on those issues; don't simply respond to whatever is in front of you.
- Don't send an e-mail unless absolutely necessary, and resist the

temptation to copy people who have no "need to know."

- Work off-site from time to time if your employer and work situation allow it.

Recognition of the potential adverse effects of the electronic bombardment that we all weather on a daily basis is the first step in dealing with the problem. Consciously and consistently creating time to focus and concentrate is the solution.

– CHAPTER TWENTY-ONE –
FRAME THE CHALLENGE CORRECTLY

"The test of a first-rate intelligence is the ability to hold two opposite ideas in mind at the same time and still retain the ability to function."

– F. Scott Fitzgerald

In 1989, the venerable book publisher Encyclopedia Britannica generated $627 million in revenues by selling hard-bound encyclopedias priced at $1,300 per set. A mere five years later, sales had plummeted to less than $300 million. Other producers of encyclopedias had captured huge chunks of Britannica's market share by introducing CD-ROM options that allowed customers to peruse articles in a more interesting, flexible, and cheaper way. Britannica had been slow to adopt the new digital technology for the primary reason that it viewed itself as a book seller, rather than as a purveyor of knowledge and information that might be sold in many different forms. Company leadership stubbornly persisted in holding onto a frame for understanding its business that was woefully outdated. By the time Britannica recognized its mistake and took steps to recover, it nearly imploded. Leadership had failed miserably in one of its most fundamental responsibilities: the requirement to frame the challenge correctly.

What is a frame? Succinctly put, frames help us to simplify reality. Frames enable us to make sense of and understand the complex world that surrounds us. They are assumptions we make that allow us to determine how to expend our energy, what to focus on, and what to ignore. According to scholar Marvin L. Minsky, "The terms *frame* and *framing* have their origin in cognitive science and artificial intelligence…. and refer to the mental representations that allow humans to perceive, interpret, judge, choose, and act." The way that we frame a problem or a challenge has a potentially huge impact on how we communicate, approach solutions and, ultimately, make decisions. We all use frames constantly and they are incredibly important in facilitating our day-to-day functioning.

The problem lies in the fact that frames sometimes cause tunnel vision. We can become trapped in overly rigid frames. In short, as the leadership team at Encyclopedia Britannica so painfully discovered, frames can be occasionally dead wrong in ways that ultimately prove disastrous.

The words leaders use to communicate framing to their followers matter greatly. Studies demonstrate that even slight changes in the wording of a problem or challenge can have a significant impact on the way people respond. For example, a well-known study by Daniel Kahneman and Amos Tversky highlights the importance of decision frames. The researchers found that people are more inclined to take higher risks if a decision is framed with emphasis on a potential loss. Conversely, if a decision is framed with a positive emphasis on potential gain people tend to think more broadly and take fewer unnecessary chances. These results are true even when the practical outcome in either case is the same.

In one experiment, people were more clear-thinking and risk averse when presented with a decision framed in terms of the odds that lives would be saved (gains) with a particular medical treatment, versus the same scenario that emphasized deaths (losses) that would be prevented.

Further studies demonstrate that entire organizations — just like the individuals who comprise them — tend to act more rigidly when a challenge is framed as a threat. When the problem is posed as an opportunity, organizations display more flexible and adaptive behavior.

There is also more recent evidence that when an issue is posed first as a threat, but then reframed as an opportunity, organizations display better skill in their problem-solving. For example, the newspaper industry generally first viewed the Internet as a threat. Subsequently, the most successful newspapers came to reframe the challenge posed by the Internet as a potential opportunity to try new things, and allocated resources accordingly. Consciously working to create new, more positive frames is therefore frequently a good way to arrive at well-conceived solutions.

How can you as a leader achieve better results in framing issues?

- Avoid forcing your frame on the team. There are times when it is appropriate to hold back and allow for healthy give-and-take before asserting your point of view.

- Be constantly aware of and question your own frames. Ask yourself what in your background and experience is causing you to hold a particular frame.

- Work to understand the frames of others. Listen carefully to what they say. Ask yourself what in their background and experience is driving their world view. What can you learn from developing a better appreciation of their frames?

- Talk about your frames and have an open and honest conversation with your team about the assumptions you are making, either individually or as a team.

- Use words carefully. Pose problems in a way that accentuates the positive, and potential gains, rather than the negative, and potential losses.

- In the alternative, pose problems in a way that allows competing frames (reflecting both potential threats and opportunities) to surface. Or adopt multiple frames simultaneously when analyzing a problem. Consider the situation from many different points of view. Do whatever is required to help you and your team question your own frames and think more broadly.

- Keep your frames in front of you during the entire decision-making process. Ask yourself how your thinking might change at any point along the way if your frames were to change.

In the end, framing is a complex skill that requires awareness and discipline. In the book *Wharton on Making Decisions*, business school professors Paul Schoemaker and J. Edward Russo summarize, "Ultimately, this is where management differs from leadership. Managers operate within an existing frame and execute; leaders ask the deeper questions, provoke new ideas and operate across frames, moving the organization from an old frame to a new one. Effective leaders challenge old frames, envision bold new ones, and contrast the two very clearly." Framing the challenge correctly, difficult though it may be, can mean the difference between success and failure in the incredibly complex world in which we live and work.

— CHAPTER TWENTY-TWO —
ENGAGE IN
CONSTRUCTIVE
CONFLICT

"Avoid fight or flight.
Talk through differences."

– Stephen Covey

In July 2009, Ursula Burns became the new CEO of Xerox, taking over from Anne Mulcahy. Mulcahy had led the venerable technology company since 2000, and with a steady hand had guided it from the brink of disaster to relative stability. But a great deal of work remains to be done. Among other things, investors are now looking for continued improvements in revenue and earnings. One of the key cultural challenges, identified by Burns in a recent feature in the *New York Times*, is what she calls, "Terminal niceness…. We are really, really, really nice." Burns believes the "Xerox family" needs to start acting more like a real family.

Burns says, "When we're in the family, you don't have to be as nice as when you're outside of the family. I want us to stay civil and kind, but we have to be frank — and the reason we can be frank is because we are all in the same family." Ursula Burns recognizes that in order to achieve the best possible business outcomes over time, it is critically important to create a culture in which people engage in constructive conflict.

Some leaders believe that any conflict at all is a bad thing for their teams and organizations. But conflict, when managed properly, can actually be extremely beneficial. Professor Michael Finer of the Columbia University Graduate School of Business says, "Contests over personal agendas are unhealthy, but conflicts over ideas are good." When a team argues openly and honestly over ideas, asserts Finer, the process can "lead to creativity, innovation, and positive change by squeezing the best ideas from each participant's mind."

Perceptive leaders recognize the need for frank discourse when important issues are on the line, and they use their skills to deliberately enable disagreement and debate. Says Finer, "The higher the stakes in any key decision, the more vital it is to stimulate this healthy kind of conflict."

Mediation expert Mark Gerzon uses a cooking analogy to describe how talented leaders manage the process of conflict. A situation in which there is no conflict at all is akin to cooking with a temperature that is too cold. Nothing happens. The chef needs to turn up the temperature a bit — but not too hot, because excessive heat can result in an overcooked dish. Similarly, leaders need to ensure that there is enough heat in the debate to achieve a good result, but not so much that the exchange boils over into a negative, unhealthy fight. Like Goldilocks in the story of the three bears, good leaders need to use their experience in managing conflict to find the temperature that is "just right."

Professor Finer encourages leaders to think of good conflict vs. bad in the same way we think of good cholesterol vs. bad. He says, "Once you compare the negative impact of bad cholesterol on your health with the benefits of good cholesterol, you'll likely feel more motivated to change the way you're doing things. You adopt whatever discipline and practices — new fitness or dietary regimens — you need to reduce the bad kind and increase the good kind." Business leaders who can favorably manipulate both kinds of conflict and develop habits that put an emphasis on the good will be able to save their companies from "having a corporate coronary."

There are a number of techniques for managing bad conflict when it happens. Focusing on facts and ideas rather than emotions and personalities is key. Encouraging a compromise that results in a fair solution or a collaboration that results in a joint recommendation are also tools in a good leader's kit.

Good leaders also work hard to maximize positive conflict. They are clear about roles, responsibilities, and expected outcomes in the decision-making process. They listen carefully to the entire debate and avoid stating their own opinion up front, as that may result in groupthink. They may encourage role-playing to stimulate debate, for example, by having some members of the team play the role of the company's chief competitor. They may assign a person to deliberately play the role of the devil's advocate.

Good leaders ask non-threatening, open-ended questions. They ask people what they are thinking and how they are feeling. They call upon the quiet people in a discussion to make sure everyone has a chance to be heard. Professor Finer says the leaders who use these techniques send the message, "I want your ideas. I want your disagreement. I want you to challenge me."

When Ursula Burns took over at Xerox, she spoke to a group of employees and described the all-too common phenomenon of the meeting where some people talk and others just listen: "We know it. We know what we do… And then the meeting ends, and we leave and go, 'Man, that wasn't true.' I'm like, "Why didn't you say that in the meeting?'" Burns is determined to create a culture in which people are unafraid to speak the truth in the attempt to produce good business results. She insists that Xerox will never achieve true greatness again until the day the company learns to do what any strong, healthy family does: consistently, openly, and honestly engage in constructive conflict.

– CHAPTER TWENTY-THREE –
AVOID THE TYRANNY OF MEETINGS

"The length of a meeting rises with the number of people present and the productiveness of a meeting falls with the square of the number of people present."

– Eileen Shanahan

In a classic Dilbert cartoon, a group of co-workers sits down around a conference table and the group leader says, "There is no specific agenda for this meeting. As usual, we'll just make unrelated emotional statements about things that bother us." In that spirit, I'm about to make an emotional statement about something that has bothered me throughout my career, which is the excessive number of interminable, meandering, useless meetings that take place in the corporate culture. I strongly encourage any of my friends and colleagues in business (who are willing to listen) to avoid the tyranny of meetings whenever possible.

I once worked in a retail store where, at the beginning of each day, the general manager would pull his leadership team together for a meeting which lasted, literally, all morning. It was not a discussion with give and take, but rather a chance for him to go on about any subject that popped into his head. Then, meeting complete, he would walk the sales floor with those same leaders and get genuinely angry when he saw problems in their respective areas. Evidently, he thought we each had a clone that was getting the work done while he blathered on. It was surreal, and the very definition of the tyranny of meetings at work.

Later in my career, I also spent many hours in meetings where the primary objective was to discuss the fact that we spent too many hours in meetings. It was sort of like being in the U.S. Congress and serving as a member of the Committee on Committees.

In the June 2009 issue of *Inc.* magazine, entrepreneur Joel Spolsky discussed how the culture of Microsoft, where he worked in the early 1990's, has changed in the years since he left. Then, Microsoft employed about 10,000 people worldwide and was headquartered in Redmond, Washington, on a campus of a dozen buildings within easy walking distance of one another. Now, there are 90,000 employees globally, and the corporate headquarters comprise 94 buildings. A fleet of company-owned vehicles transports people from place to place on campus.

Most notably, at the new Microsoft, meetings have proliferated. Spolsky says, "Back in my day, meetings were avoided like the plague, and it was considered a burden if you had to go to three or four a week. But today, the average Microsoft manager is scheduled to within an inch of his or her life. The new virtue is keeping a schedule of brisk half-hour meetings, and most of the mid-level managers... [have] consecutive half-hour meetings scheduled for stretches of days at a time."

Though Microsoft's business has understandably suffered like most others in today's recessionary economy, one wonders whether bloated bureaucracy (Spolsky describes the comical series of registration steps he was required to go through just to access the free Wi-Fi network as a guest on Microsoft's campus) and the new "meeting culture" have contributed to relatively poor recent performance by Microsoft, in comparison to the leaner, more carefree days gone by.

With that said, there are clearly times when meetings are appropriate and very necessary. Often, the results that can be achieved in a face-to-face sit-down vastly exceed what can be accomplished through a phone conversation, conference call, or e-mail. Every culture is different, and no set of guidelines applies in every circumstance, but here are some basic tips for meeting organizers that might help improve the quality of your meetings and thereby increase productivity:

- Invite the right people. If the invitees to your meeting do not have the requisite experience, technical knowledge, or decision-making authority, you have wasted everyone's time.

- Start and stop the meeting on time. This will force discipline and eliminate meandering. Assign a timekeeper who has the courage to speak up when things get off track.

- Develop a detailed agenda beforehand and share it at the beginning of the meeting. It should contain specific, actionable outcomes. It should answer the questions: Why are we here and what do we intend to accomplish?

- Assign a note taker. The note taker should review key points before the end of the meeting to ensure consensus on what was discussed, and then distribute notes to all stakeholders after the meeting, including those who may have missed the meeting.

- Stick to the agenda. Don't be inflexible, but try to limit unnecessary digressions and stay on task.
- Use real data, not anecdote or emotion. Remain factual in your approach.
- Allow and encourage everyone to contribute. Listen carefully to what each team member says, even if you disagree.
- Create an environment in which people are comfortable speaking up if they do disagree. Encourage open and honest debate. Thoroughly discuss key points of difference.
- At the end, summarize meeting outcomes and assign next steps. Be specific and make sure each person knows what is expected of him/her going forward.

What is the culture of your company, organization, or team concerning meetings? Do you have too many, not enough, or just the right number of meetings? Are your meetings well-organized and efficient? Do you lose productivity with too much time wasted talking about getting work done, instead of actually doing the work? Do you have time to think and reflect in your job? If you are less than perfect in your meeting disciplines, please consider trying some of the above-described techniques. If you do, you will go a long way toward avoiding that dread corporate disease that saps energy and hinders results: the tyranny of meetings.

– CHAPTER TWENTY-FOUR –
USE THE POWER OF STORIES

*"Words are how we think;
stories are how we link."*

– Christina Baldwin

When I was young, my maternal grandmother, who was the God-fearing wife of a Baptist preacher and lived to the wise old age of 100 years, used to read to me before bedtime from her well-worn *Holy Bible* (King James version). My favorite story from the Old Testament, and one that I insisted she read to me over and over, was the saga of David and Goliath. Because I too was small in stature, I could identify with the plight of the diminutive David as he fearlessly confronted the gigantic and intimidating Goliath.

To this day, nearly five decades later, the hair on my neck still stands up when I consider the words: "And it came to pass, when the Philistine arose, and came and drew nigh to meet David, that David hasted, and ran toward the army to meet the Philistine…. And David put his hand in his bag, and took thence a stone, and slang it, and smote the Philistine in the forehead…. So David prevailed over the Philistine with a sling and with a stone…. there was no sword in the hand of David…" I have never forgotten the beauty of the language or the power of this story and its timeless lesson that with courage, insight, and perseverance, great odds can be overcome. Underdogs who believe in themselves can triumph in the end, just like the intrepid shepherd boy who became the famous King David.

Stories are one of the oldest and most fundamental forms of human communication. In the distant past, before history could be written down, oral traditions served to pass knowledge, wisdom, and cultural norms from one generation to the next. Today, even as in biblical times, great leaders understand and use the power of stories to teach and inspire their followers.

In her book, *Whoever Tells the Best Story Wins*, business consultant and author Annette Simmons says, "A story is a narration of events that simulates a visual, sensory, and emotional experience that feels significant for both the listener and the teller. If experience is the best teacher, then story is second-best." Simmons argues that while tools for data gathering and measurement of results have improved significantly, corporate leaders fail to adequately grasp the subjective side of business. She states, "Business success is a function of both facts and feelings."

Harvard Business School professor and leadership expert John Kotter would agree. In a 2006 article from *Forbes* magazine entitled "The Power of Stories," Kotter writes, "Over the years I have become convinced that we learn best — and change — from hearing stories that strike a chord within us.... As I look around me today, I see that too few business leaders grasp the idea that stories can have a profound effect on people.... Those in leadership positions who fail to grasp or use the power of stories risk failure for their companies and for themselves."

But the best leaders are not only skilled storytellers who comprehend the power of compelling narratives to teach; they also know that their own actions and behaviors can generate stories that may (or may not) serve to create better business outcomes for the organizations that they lead.

Lou Gerstner became CEO of the unwieldy and insular behemoth IBM in 1993. The stories that almost immediately came to be told about him made it apparent to everyone that dramatic change was about to take place. For example, in a culture where meetings consisted of presenting dreary reams of information on endless slides via overhead projector, Gerstner shut the projector off and initiated a conversational dialogue instead. Painful though the transition became, Gerstner is credited with pulling off one of the most dramatic turnarounds in corporate history and saving IBM, in significant part because he appreciated the power of stories to transform a culture.

Annette Simmons reminds us, "Story has the power to fill in between the lines, to breathe feelings of human *experience* into outcomes, strategic plans, and objective goals so people can see, hear, and feel enough for it to feel real. Once a goal feels real in their imagination, people are much more likely to do what it takes to make it real in the physical world. They not only understand the what, they have a feeling for the how and the why."

Do you as a leader understand the fundamental truth that through stories, both individuals and entire teams can comprehend the world more clearly and engage more effectively in achieving the purpose of your organization? Do you use stories as "teachable moments" that can improve understanding, encourage creativity, and increase motivation?

Just as important, what are the stories that are told about you as a leader and about your organization? Are they the stories that you would wish to be shared among your employees, customers, and shareholders? If not, then consider the actions you need to take to generate a better, more positive story. Remember Annette Simmons's insightful words, "As the ambiguity of business and life continues to become more apparent, we will find that our ability to understand subjectivity and to alter subjective feelings will become more important. In other words, whoever tells the best story wins."

– Part Four–
Relationships

*"Remember, we all stumble, every one of us.
That's why it's a comfort to go hand in hand."*

– Emily Kimbrough

— CHAPTER TWENTY-FIVE —
GREAT TEAMS NEVER GIVE IN

"... and a little child shall lead them."

– Isaiah 11:6

Great teams never give in. In business, as in sports or any other human endeavor, the very best teams simply refuse to be defeated. I was reminded of this fact several years ago when I had the honor of coaching my daughter Lucia and her second and third grade peers in basketball. Basketball, like business, is a fast-paced, rough-and-tumble game that involves lots of strategy and, in order to win, requires skill and determination from its participants. At least at the highest levels of the sport, this is true.

But for Luci and her pals, practices consisted mostly of social time, laughing, doing each other's hair, taking bathroom breaks together en masse, and some basketball. I tried to teach basic fundamentals with a focus on teamwork. I thought they were listening, but I was never sure. They took a vote and decided to call themselves the "Hot Peppers." I was not crazy about this team name, but went along. Did I mention the laughter?

This was a middling team, at best. During the regular season we might have won a couple more games than we lost, but no one predicted greatness for this team.

But in the annual year-end tournament that determines the over-all league champion, something came over the Peppers. They pulled together as a unit and demonstrated, almost heroically, that great teams never give in.

There was a team that had dominated the schedule all year long. This team had several girls who were big, strong, and talented. They wore aqua jerseys, and my 8-year-old daughter referred to them simply (and somewhat in awe) as, "the team that is the color of aqua." This team had beaten the Peppers soundly and gone undefeated in the regular season, but somehow the Peppers had gotten through the preliminary rounds of the tournament to face this mighty foe in the championship game.

I knew we were up against it, but wasn't sure if the girls knew. I did not want to invoke the Holy Bible and cite David and Goliath but, trust me, my thoughts went there. Instead, I recalled a recent Super Bowl game, where a lowly underdog had defeated the mighty favorite.

"Did you girls see the Super Bowl?"

"Yes."

"Who won?"

"The team that wasn't supposed to win."

"Right."

The Peppers went out and fought hard. They were behind most of the game. But suddenly, the team that was the color of aqua started to play not to lose. They sat back on their heels. They made mistakes. They even panicked a bit near the end. The Peppers came back.

Pretty soon, with no time left, one of our little gals stepped up to the free throw line, score tied 15-15, with a chance to win the game. First shot missed. Second shot hit the back rim, bounced straight up, and came down through the hoop. Pandemonium erupted. The Peppers had triumphed. Dairy Queen beckoned.

What are the ingredients that go into creating a team with this kind of capability? The first is leadership. And not just leadership of the obvious kind, as important as that is, from the head coach or the team leader in business. Leadership can come from any person, at any time. Our final couple of baskets came from one of our best athletes, who had played a quiet game up to that point. Isn't it amazing how often your top performers seem to come through, demonstrating leadership in the clutch?

The second ingredient is skill. Several girls on the Peppers, silliness aside, could put the rock in the hole when they felt like it. This is where hard work, repetition, and practice together as a unit come in. These are essential fundamentals in business, just as they are in sports.

Finally, there is the most important ingredient, and the most difficult one to describe. Call it team chemistry, call it trust and confidence, call it swagger, call it what you will. A truly great team believes in itself in a way that is palpable. You can see it in the way such a team carries itself, interacts together and, ultimately, performs.

We are in difficult times right now, but teams that possess that magical combination of leadership, skill, and chemistry will survive the trial. They will emerge stronger than they were before.

What will your team do in this economy? Will you play not to lose? Will you let events dictate what happens to you? Will you sit back? Will panic set in? Or will you look each other confidently in the eye, take control, count on your leaders, work hard together, trust each other, and snatch victory from the jaws of defeat? This decision cannot be postponed.

In 1941, amidst the throes of World War II and as the fate of his nation hung in peril, British Prime Minister Winston Churchill addressed the students at Harrow School, his alma mater, outside London. He told them, "Never give in. Never give in. Never, never, never, never- in nothing great or small, large or petty- never give in...." That was good advice for young people during dark days, but isn't it interesting how young people can sometimes teach us too?

Occasionally, when I face a moment of truth in today's tumultuous world I think back, smile, and whisper to myself, "Remember the Peppers. Never give in."

– CHAPTER TWENTY-SIX –
PREPARE AND ADAPT AS A TEAM

"A team is not a bunch of people with job titles, but a congregation of individuals, each of whom has a role that is understood by other members."

– Meredith Belbin

In late 1911, two teams of intrepid explorers, one led by the Norwegian Roald Amundsen, the other by the British naval officer Robert Falcon Scott, raced to see who would be first to arrive at the South Pole. Amundsen achieved the Pole on December 14 and returned safely with all hands alive and well. Scott's team reached the Pole five weeks later, but every man in the party (Scott and four others) perished on the return trip.

These two leaders and their respective teams represented profoundly different styles and approaches. One group experienced triumph, and the other tragedy. In the end, Amundsen and his hardy band of Scandinavians — in a way that is extremely relevant to today's business leaders — demonstrated the critical need to prepare and adapt as a team.

In what was known as the "heroic age" of Antarctic exploration during the 1890s and early 1900s, the South Pole constituted the ultimate prize. To reach the Pole would be seen as an accomplishment akin to landing men on the moon in the 1960s. Though the frigid, ice-covered Antarctic continent had been explored extensively for many decades, no one had yet reached the South Pole when Amundsen, Scott, and their respective teams set out to win the right to call themselves the first to claim the coveted objective.

Amundsen decided at an early age that he would be a polar explorer and prepared an entire lifetime for the ultimate test of his abilities. He recognized the knowledge and skills he would need to succeed and set out with great determination to acquire them. He was descended from seafaring men, and so first he became a master mariner. He became physically fit and an expert skier. To achieve polar experience, he read every source he could find on the subject, and volunteered as an unpaid mate to accompany an Antarctic expedition in 1896.

Amundsen led a voyage from 1903 to 1906 that became the first to successfully sail the Northwest Passage between the Atlantic and Pacific oceans. During this trip he befriended local Netsilik Eskimos, learning their language and studying their culture in detail. The knowledge he gained about clothing, hunting, dog-handling and survival skills served him well in adapting to the polar environment he would subsequently encounter. In a fascinating book on the race to the Pole, *The Last Place on Earth*, author Roland Huntford writes, "There are very few civilized men — even today — who can immerse themselves in a primitive culture without trying to improve on it. Amundsen had set out with perception and humility to learn from anyone who had something to teach."

Amundsen was an outstanding leader as well. Huntford describes life aboard Amundsen's ship *Gjoa*, where each individual was treated as a professional who was there to share in the work and help achieve a common goal: "Respect was given not to rank, but to the man… One pilot said that Amundsen's ship was the most astonishing he had ever seen. 'No orders were given, but everyone seemed to know what to do.'" Amundsen chose his team carefully and prepared and trained them rigorously — just as he had himself — for their ordeal.

In contrast, Robert Falcon Scott represented the epitome of the rigid, unimaginative officer caste of the British navy. Scott was ambitious for no one but himself, and appears to have pursued polar exploration for the primary reason than that it would expedite his promotion to higher levels within the navy. Scott was a mediocre leader. Huntford writes of life aboard Scott's ship, "The picture that emerges is one of an insecure, unhappy, emotional disciplinarian…" Scott was also unwilling to learn: "His Naval training had taught him form, discipline, obedience, but stifled independent thought. He lacked capacity to learn from experience."

In pursuit of the South Pole, Amundsen's team relied primarily on highly efficient dog teams for transportation. Scott's team brought some dogs, but was unskilled in their use. Instead, Scott's men manhauled their equipment and also used three motor sledges, one of which fell through the ice while the other two failed early in the expedition. Scott also brought ponies that were extremely ill-suited to the extreme conditions.

Amundsen's men were able to ski, but Scott's group lacked training as skiers. Amundsen marked his route and laid supply depots carefully. Scott's approach was more haphazard. Amundsen ensured sufficient supplies of food and fuel. Scott miscalculated in this critical requirement.

Huntford concludes, "Scott marched off into the unknown, singularly ill-prepared. Beyond a hazy hope of reaching the Pole, he had no plans of campaign.... He thought snow and ice could be overcome by brute force. He did not understand the world he had chosen to invade." The result was that Scott and his men, courageous though they were, died from hunger, exhaustion, and exposure on the return trip from the Pole.

Amundsen and team had meticulously prepared for and adapted to the harsh environment they faced. Scott's team failed to acknowledge hard reality and stumbled forward, grossly unprepared, in hopes that the world would adapt to them.

In today's tough economic environment, are you and your team prepared for the extreme challenges you will face? Do you appreciate and adapt to your situation as it really exists, or are you hoping that the external world will change to fit your current operational model? The simple truth is that teams that prepare and adapt with the most skill will best weather today's storm of economic uncertainty.

— CHAPTER TWENTY-SEVEN —
BE GENERATIONALLY SAVVY

"From now on, change will be the constant.
The individuals best prepared to succeed are
those who can learn, modify, and grow,
regardless of age, experience, or ego."

– Danny Goodman

"The children now love luxury; they have bad manners, contempt for authority; they show disrespect for elders and love chatter in place of exercise. Children are now tyrants, not the servants of their households. They no longer rise when elders enter the room. They contradict their parents, chatter before company, gobble up dainties at the table, cross their legs, and tyrannize their teachers." This quotation is attributed to the great Greek philosopher Socrates, who lived in the fifth century BC.

I have two wonderful teenage daughters. They are not perfect — nor, as they would be quick to point out, is their dad — but on the whole they are bright, energetic, industrious, and competent, as are their many friends (with just a few exceptions). Unlike Socrates, I do not despair for a future that rests in the hands of the next generation. But I do know that my daughters have had a profoundly different life experience from me. As young people come into the workforce in increasing numbers, good business leaders must learn to be generationally savvy in order to tap this vast potential and succeed over the long run.

While experts disagree on the exact cutoff of dates, in general, the different generational divides in America are defined as follows: Traditionalists were born before 1946; Baby Boomers were born from 1946 through 1964; Generation X (almost 50 million people) was born from 1965 through 1981; and Generation Y, or Millennials (more than 75 million people), were born from 1982 through 2000.

The Boomers (my subset — almost 80 million strong), have dominated and held on to power in corporate America for much of recent history but, as Bob Dylan tells us, "the times they are a-changin'." Forty percent of Boomers are currently eligible for retirement, and 77 million will retire from the workforce in the next 20 years. While some aging employees may continue to work either by choice or necessity, as consultant and author Sarah Sladek says, "It's going to be the largest turnover in human capital in human history, and many organizations are simply ill-prepared."

Savvy companies must come to grips with this pending reality and determine the steps they will take to hire, train, retain, lead, and market to the 125 million restless and ambitious members of Gens X and Y.

What are the qualities that characterize this younger generation of workers? The Xers are independent and don't want the boss looking over their shoulders. They want to be challenged by interesting work, enjoy opportunities to learn and grow on the job, and establish meaningful relationships with co-workers. They like to have fun, to be evaluated using clear metrics, and to be rewarded for achieving their goals. They appreciate flexibility, and will remain loyal to an employer as long as the employer acknowledges their contribution.

Millennials are confident high achievers who also want to find meaning, flexibility, and strong relationships in their work. They have never known a world without the wonders of technology, and tend to communicate digitally rather than face-to-face. Their parents have been very involved in their lives. A recent survey by Michigan State found that 26 percent of employers said a parent had lobbied for a job on behalf of their Millennial child, while 31 percent said a parent had submitted a resume on behalf of a child.

Some critics call the Millennials "Slackers," and suggest they have been coddled by their parents, leading to a sense of entitlement. No doubt, the Millennials want to get ahead (and quickly), but a recent survey of the other generations found that only 7 percent felt the Millennials were prepared to succeed in today's workplace. Nevertheless, Millennials are talented, well-educated, and eager to make their mark on the world.

Given these general tendencies, what can employers do? Cargill has acknowledged the desire of Gens X and Y to learn and be challenged by creating a talent development program that rotates younger workers through a series of jobs during their first year, giving them exposure to different areas of the company.

At Best Buy, where one-sixth of the workforce is between 16 and 19 years old, employees have an opportunity to invest a portion of their paycheck into social causes that are important to them. Best Buy also encourages digital connectivity through its in-house social networking platform known as "Blue Shirt Nation." Employees are encouraged to submit questions and ideas to anyone in the company, all the way up to the CEO.

The accounting firm Deloitte has created a Mass Career Customization (MCC) program in response to employees clamoring for better work-life balance. With MCC, workers are allowed to focus not just on career goals but on life goals as well, and to pursue lateral as well as upward mobility. This represents a shift from the traditional "up-or-out" model, and encourages employees to find meaning in their work in balance with healthy personal lives.

And what about the Boomers? We are not done yet. Interestingly, data suggests that Boomers and Yers (who sandwich the significantly less numerous Gen Xers) share some important traits in common. A recent *Harvard Business Review* article states, "Both Boomers and Gen Ys want to contribute to society through their labor; seek flexible working arrangements; value social connections at work and loyalty to a company; and prize other rewards of employment over monetary compensation."

So, apparently, despite our very different life experiences, we Boomers share more in common with our Millennial children than meets the eye. The employers that are generationally savvy understand this reality and will succeed over the long haul by creating work environments that are fun, flexible, and challenging for workers of every age group.

– CHAPTER TWENTY-EIGHT –
TRUST AND RELATIONSHIPS MATTER

"Business is not just doing deals; business is having great products, doing great engineering, and providing tremendous service to customers. Finally, business is a cobweb of human relationships."

– H. Ross Perot

Every positive thing that has ever happened to me in my professional career has come out of a personal relationship. I have never gotten a job, received a promotion, or switched organizations without the help of someone I knew and trusted, and who knew and trusted me. The dysfunctional and poor performing teams that I have been a part of (unfortunately, there have been a few) have failed precisely because human relationships broke down, or were never properly established in the first place. I repeatedly tell my two teenage daughters, who will soon enter the workforce, to remember this essential truth: in business, as in life, trust and relationships matter.

Linda Easley, president and chief executive of the Columbus, Ohio-based retailer The Limited, emphasizes the importance of this principle from the very first days that a person starts a job on her team. When asked recently what she tells new managers who come to work for her, she responded, "I tell them: 'Take the first 90 days. The relationships you build in your first few months here are critical to your success. Try not to talk in meetings. I know you're going to want to demonstrate that you're really capable and you deserve to be here by showing your smarts. But if you listen and let the void fill with what's around you, you'll learn a ton.'"

Stephen Sadove, chairman and chief executive of Saks Inc., also spoke recently of the importance of relationships in crafting his successful career. When asked about his most fundamental leadership lessons he says, "I've used opportunities to get involved and develop relationships with a diverse set of people as opposed to the narrow group of people I was dealing with day-to-day, and that made a huge difference. It shaped my philosophy in terms of the importance of relationship-building, and how to run a business." He goes on to say, "I obviously work with business issues, but I try to go out of my way in mentoring, coaching and developing young people. I tend to care a lot about the people and the relationships that they have, how the team is operating, the culture." Sadove concludes, "I've been amazed over the years how relationships that come out of one thing go toward something else. If you give positive vibes, if you show an interest, by and large a lot of people will react."

Indeed, the importance of the tone and example set by top leadership cannot be overstated. But relationships at every level within an organization matter as well. In a well-known *Harvard Business Re-*

view article entitled "Eight Ways to Build Collaborative Teams," business scholars Lynda Gratton and Tamara Erickson provide practical suggestions for leaders who need to enable complex teams (those that are large, virtual, diverse, and specialized) execute major initiatives within their organizations. Among other recommendations, the authors' research shows that in order to maximize performance:

- Top executives must work to build and maintain social relationships throughout their companies. For example, the Royal Bank of Scotland built a headquarters that features an indoor atrium which purposefully puts employees into close contact with one another on a daily basis, encouraging social interaction and collaboration.

- Top leadership also needs to personally model strong relationships and a cooperative, people-focused culture. Teams are very in tune to the example set from above.

- Team leaders should, if possible, ensure that some members of a new team already know each other. At Nokia, when skills must move from one business unit to another, entire small teams are transferred, rather than shuffling individuals. This ensures cohesion and more open knowledge-sharing.

- Those who lead complex teams should focus first on articulating the task at hand, but as the project goes forward emphasize the importance of relationship-building. If a team knows and trusts one another, when inevitable conflict arises, problems can be much more easily resolved.

Sometimes, relationship-building is incredibly difficult. But those who persevere in developing trust and establishing connections even under challenging circumstances will prevail over time. In 1998, Gary Loveman moved from a position in academe to take over as chief operating officer of the casino company Harrah's. Insiders resented Loveman and felt that several internal candidates were more deserving of the job. Loveman knew he would have a particularly difficult time with the chief financial officer, whose support and expertise he desperately needed. Loveman worked especially hard to win the favor of this individual, conferring with him frequently, sharing information, and including him in meetings and decision making. At least in part out of his focus on the importance of this key relationship and others, Loveman was named CEO of Harrah's in 2003.

Does your organization promote a culture that values the social side of life, and that emphasizes the quality of daily human interactions? Are relationships important at your company? Do you have at least one good friend in your workplace? Do you as a leader understand how critical it is to know and trust your team members? Do you work to build relationships even when it is hard to do? Some might argue that the answers to these questions pertain more to the "soft" side of business and, therefore, are not important. But those leaders and organizations who understand the basic truth that trust and relationships matter know better.

– CHAPTER TWENTY-NINE –
CHERISH THE MAVERICK

"The whole world loves a maverick and the whole world wants the maverick to achieve something nobler than simple rebellion."

– Kevin Patterson

Samuel A. Maverick was a nineteenth-century Texas lawyer, legislator, and landowner. He was a political progressive who was a signatory of the Texas Declaration of Independence. As a rancher, Maverick refused to brand his cattle for the stated reason that he felt the practice was cruel to the animals. His detractors asserted that he failed to brand his cattle so that he could gather up any unbranded animals and claim them as his own. Other sources argued that he simply had no interest in ranching, and avoided branding only out of general indifference. Whichever story is true, when friends and neighbors saw an unbranded calf or yearling roaming the range they would say, "Those are mavericks." The term "maverick" soon came to take on a different meaning, defined by the *Oxford English Dictionary* as "An unorthodox or independent-minded person."

We all know unorthodox or independent-minded people. We may even be such a person ourselves. In a business setting, mavericks are fascinating because despite their quirks, they often add enormous value to the enterprises they serve as a result of their unconventional way of seeing the world. In the alternative, mavericks are also sometimes a royal pain in the rear end. Those organizations that learn to cherish the maverick — while simultaneously managing that person — tend to be successful over time because they are open to different approaches and constant change.

Lieutenant Colonel Earl Hancock "Pete" Ellis was arguably the all-time maverick in the United States Marine Corps, a venerable organization with a long history of colorful characters. Few officers had a greater impact on Marine history, but Ellis is largely unknown today.

Pete Ellis served in the Marines from 1900 to 1923, and came to be regarded during the First World War (while working as a staff officer) as a genius at military planning. It was between the World Wars, however, that Ellis made his greatest contribution. In 1920 he authored an eighty-page study called "Advanced Base Operations in Micronesia," which set out "To guide and coordinate training and activities of the Marine Corps in peacetime so as to be ready to execute war plans." The document prophetically anticipated a Japanese attack that would necessitate a need for advance bases to support the American naval fleet. Further, Ellis correctly predicted the Japanese fleet would remain in its home waters until an anticipated meeting engagement with the American fleet. Finally, Japanese aggression would require a response in the form of an amphibious island-hopping campaign in the Central Pacific Ocean, to be carried out by none other than the United States Marine Corps.

"Advanced Base Operations in Micronesia" became the template for the U.S. military campaign in the Pacific during World War II. Many people came to think of Ellis not only as an incredibly far-sighted strategist and naval theorist, but as "the father of amphibious warfare."

Unfortunately, Pete Ellis did not live long enough to see his ideas come into fruition. Like many mavericks, he possessed a dark side. Ellis was prone to alcoholism and depression, and behaved in occasionally bizarre ways. On one occasion while stationed in the Philippines, after a particularly boring dinner with the post chaplain, an inebriated Ellis shot the dinner plates off the table with his service revolver.

As his career languished because of such incidents, Ellis volunteered in 1923 to go on a secret mission to expose suspected Japanese fortifications in Micronesia, and to gather intelligence for his proposed island-hopping campaign. Ellis failed in his objectives and died a mysterious death on Palau Island, in the Caroline Islands. Some people argued he was murdered as a spy by the Japanese, but the weight of evidence demonstrates that he drank himself to death.

Outrageous behavior aside, Ellis enjoyed the support during the prime of his career of many influential superiors, including Marine Commandant General John A. Lejeune. These officers overlooked Ellis's flaws and encouraged him in his brilliance. When told once that "Colonel Ellis was indisposed," General Lejeune responded, "Ellis drunk is better than anyone else around here sober." While Ellis's superiors undoubtedly should have done more than just cover up his problems and instead reached out to help him, it is nevertheless true that he was purposefully put in position to make a significant contribution despite his many shortcomings.

While dangerous and extreme conduct is never excusable, what about the maverick who is neither dangerous nor extreme but merely different? I have worked in organizations that purported to value the maverick, but then made it incredibly difficult for that person to function and contribute because he or she refused to conform to company culture or "play nice with the other kids."

Sometimes, the boss himself or herself is a maverick — think eBay under Meg Whitman, Apple under Steve Jobs, or Oracle under Larry Ellison. These companies make it easier for mavericks to survive and thrive because unconventional thinking happens from the top on down and is deeply embedded in the genetic makeup. But sometimes, on the other hand, unoriginal approaches at the top lead to unoriginal results throughout the team.

Where does your organization stand with respect to mavericks? Do you value them for their uniqueness and their potential, if given a chance, to contribute at a high level? Do you work to manage their occasionally odd behaviors while simultaneously channeling the good energy? Or do you shut them down and push them out? Or even worse, never hire them in the first place? Organizations with the courage to cherish and the patience to manage their mavericks will realize the benefit of seeing and engaging the world in new and perhaps even prophetic ways.

– CHAPTER THIRTY –
KNOW WHERE POWER RESIDES

*"I've been promoted to middle management.
I never thought I'd sink so low."*

– Tim Gould

I have for many years held a theory about where real power resides in organizations. When I want to know about the political complexities of a company, the morale of employees, or prospects for the future, I don't talk to a powerful manager. I talk to his or her executive assistant.

I am being only slightly facetious in this observation. It is amazing how out of touch some high-level leaders become, while the people who work for them — sometimes at many layers below — have a much better grasp on what is actually taking place day-to-day within their organizations. Therefore, because I want the true scoop (and more important, because it is the right way to treat people) I am always nice to the executive assistants of the world.

Successful leaders understand that power, knowledge, and the ability to get things done in their business does not always reside exclusively with those nearest the top of the org chart, who own the longest tenures, the mightiest titles, and the fanciest offices. Good leaders strive to make sure that people are engaged at every level within the organization and valued for their potential contribution. These leaders know that employees who feel powerless in their jobs can drag an entire culture down, negatively affecting bottom-line results in countless ways that are subtle yet profound. Beyond this, the best leaders proactively work to build their own and their organization's networks by identifying those individuals (regardless of rank or title) who can help them achieve good business outcomes.

Common sense tells us that the higher one rises in any organization, the greater his or her level of engagement, sense of responsibility, and power to accomplish results. To the contrary, however, a recent study by business school professor Michael Segalla paints a different picture of reality. Segalla surveyed more than 3,000 managers, ranking them on three key dimensions based on their answers to the following questions:

1) Sense of responsibility: How much responsibility do you think you have?

2) Hierarchy: Where do you fall in the org chart?

3) Objective authority: Do you have the authority to hire, fire, and set salaries, budgets, and strategies — or have a strong say in those decisions?

Segalla then plotted individual organizational power based on the three dimensions, and his results revealed a significant number of underengaged managers, sometimes at a frighteningly high level within the various businesses surveyed. In addition, the study also identified untapped potential in the form of highly engaged managers at a low level within the hierarchy. Finally, power centers sometimes existed in unexpected places, such as branch offices away from corporate headquarters.

Segalla's conclusions and recommendations include working to identify "deadwood" within the team in the form of disengaged malcontents who hold real power, and addressing signs of trouble quickly. Highly committed employees, especially those at lower levels, must be trained and empowered, lest they eventually take their energy and talents elsewhere. Lastly, Segalla urges that organizations discover where their true power centers may be, so that key leaders in those locations can be developed and recognized for their contributions.

Without a dedicated effort to find committed people at every level, encourage their energy, and reward their results, organizations may experience the dread scourge of "powerlessness." In the July-August 2010 issue of *Harvard Business Review*, professor Rosabeth Moss Kanter addresses this malady, saying, "Powerlessness is particularly apparent in the middle ranks. When companies slash midlevel positions, they often increase the burden on the remaining people without increasing their efficacy and influence — a combination likely to arouse risk-averse rigidity. Hemmed in by rules and treated as unimportant, people get even by overcontrolling their own turf, demanding tribute before responding to requests. They vent frustrations on others who are even more powerless. It's like a cartoon sequence: The boss chastises a worker, who curses his wife, who yells at the child, who kicks the dog."

The subtle sabotage that powerless employees may commit

through their passive-aggressive behavior can bring an organization down. Good leaders deter this outcome by sharing information, listening carefully, treating everyone with respect, and allowing full participation in the process of identifying and achieving common goals.

The best leaders go a step further and actively work to build networks, both at a personal level and within their larger organizations. These leaders create a team of people from anywhere within the company — and sometimes from outside of the company — whom they can personally tap to provide input, feedback, and resources when, for example, a critical project needs to be completed.

They also consider the implications and benefits of bringing people together in ways that help the broader organization. Nissan CEO Carlos Ghosn saw a serious problem with rigid silos when he took over the company. In response, he developed cross-functional teams of mostly mid-level managers from many different business units who were tasked with recommending solutions to a range of problems from product design to cost containment. These committees soon became both formalized and regarded as a coveted assignment at Nissan.

Every person within an organization possesses the potential to either contribute to good outcomes, or not. Listless, discontented, disengaged employees at every level hold real power to hurt a company. On the bright side, motivated, high-energy people, also at every level, can save the day. It is the task of good leaders to understand how these dynamics work, and turn them to their advantage. If you are a leader who doesn't know where real power resides, or if you just need a refresher, step outside your office and have a conversation with your executive assistant. That person will set you straight.

— CHAPTER THIRTY-ONE —
BRING OUT THE BEST IN THE PEOPLE AROUND YOU

"One man can be a crucial ingredient on a team, but one man cannot make a team."

– Kareem Abdul-Jabbar

The two men could not have been less alike. One was a short, boisterous, cigar-chomping Jew from Brooklyn. The other was a tall, moody, intensely private African-American from Louisiana and Oakland. Yet over time, these two men found their common ground and formed a bond of friendship that became legendary.

Red Auerbach was one of the greatest coaches in the history of the National Basketball Association (N.B.A.), and Bill Russell one of the game's all-time best players. Together, they led the Boston Celtics to eleven N.B.A. championships in thirteen seasons. As chronicled in Russell's wonderful book, *Red and Me: My Coach, My Lifelong Friend*, they became devoted to each other until Auerbach's death in 2006. Perhaps the most outstanding characteristic of these two leaders was their uncanny ability to bring out the best in the people around them.

Bill Russell said of his relationship with Auerbach, "Although we came from different tribes as men, we recognized early on that as professionals we had a common agenda: to win basketball games... Our core philosophies — of how to be men, how to be professionals, how to be friends — were in tune, so we never had to talk about who we were or how to conduct ourselves. We just lived it. Over the next thirteen years, basketball set the stage for our relationship to evolve from caution, to admiration, to trust and respect, to a friendship that lasted a lifetime."

Russell joined the Celtics in 1956 and ultimately became team captain. He was especially noted for his unique ability to bring out the best in his teammates. In a review of Russell's book for the *New York Times*, former basketball star and U.S. Senator Bill Bradley wrote, "[Russell] had thought about the game and his role in it so much that it was only a matter of learning his teammates' strengths and weaknesses before he was capable of elevating their games. It is a rare player who thinks, 'How can I help my teammate help the team?' Russell and Auerbach understood that in a winning culture, selflessness is just common sense."

Russell's ability to influence the play of his teammates started, essentially, from the rock solid foundation of his own formidable skills as a player. He was a five-time league M.V.P. and physically gifted with great height and leaping ability. Beyond his obvious athletic skills, he was a true innovator on the basketball court. He focused on defense as the key to a team's morale, in a way that had never been tried before. In an era when players were coached never to leave their feet while playing defense, he became the game's preeminent shot blocker, dominating opposing offenses and forcing them to adjust to his intimidating new tactics.

Russell's sheer competitiveness also intimidated opponents, and won the respect of his teammates. Bradley said, "He wanted to win every matchup, every game, every title. He waged psychological warfare, on and off the court." Because of their high regard for Russell's outstanding ability and fierce desire to win, his teammates were very open to his energetic attempts to push them to improve their own games. He consciously studied the play of every Celtic and willed his teammates to perform to their highest potential. The result was an unprecedented string of championships.

Auerbach, too, appreciated the importance of each individual in the whole grand scheme. Bradley observed, "[Auerbach's] genius was to relate to each player individually. What worked for one player didn't work for all players." Auerbach even handled Russell differently, allowing him to rest during practice once the regular season began for purposes of keeping him fresh for an entire grueling N.B.A. campaign. Russell's teammates did not resent this preferential treatment because they knew, once the game began, no one was more committed to winning than their captain.

As a peer colleague, do you ask yourself Bill Russell's very important question: How can I help my teammate help the team? It is the rare person who does this. It starts with one's own skills and performance. Outstanding results engender credibility and respect. From this foundation, it becomes possible to help even the worst performer on the team get better. But the selflessness, motivation, and energy must be there.

As a leader, like Red Auerbach, do you understand that each member of the team needs to be led differently? Do you take time to get to know your people as individuals and to adjust your approach accordingly? Do you work to get the best out of each person on the team, taking into account their unique skills and abilities? Such a model makes life more complicated and requires time and hard work, but outstanding results will follow.

Bill Bradley won championships with the New York Knicks and he recalled the joys of being part of a team, like the Boston Celtics, where people made a concerted effort to bring out the best in each other: "… the bond among players lasts a lifetime… You never forget your teammates' loyalty and how you returned it in full measure, and how that trust and mutual respect allowed you to be a champion."

– CHAPTER THIRTY-TWO –
SHOW HUMILITY

*"Man is like to vanity: his days are as a
shadow that passeth away."*

– Psalm 144.4

George Catlett Marshall was the U.S. Army Chief of Staff during the Second World War. In that capacity, he managed the astronomical growth of America's armed forces from a tiny pre-war entity to the thirteen-million-person juggernaut that defeated Nazi Germany and Imperial Japan. After the war, Marshall became secretary of state and oversaw implementation of his namesake Marshall Plan that succeeded in rebuilding war-ravaged Europe. He went on to serve as secretary of defense and, later, as head of the American Red Cross. Despite these profound achievements during a lifetime of service, Marshall is perhaps one of the least-well-known leaders in our history.

Marshall's relative lack of name recognition today represents the natural outcome of his supreme selflessness coupled with his fierce and unwavering commitment to always putting the needs of the country first. George Marshall embodied a critical leadership trait that, unfortunately, we seldom see in sufficient measure: he showed humility.

When the Allied high command decided in 1944 to invade Europe via the Normandy beaches of France, President Franklin Roosevelt confronted a difficult choice as to who should lead such an important and complex operation. By all accounts, Marshall had earned the right to head up the effort, and very much desired the appointment. His superior leadership skills and strategic acumen were unmatched. Yet when Roosevelt asked Marshall whether he would prefer to lead the D-Day invasion or remain on duty in Washington as chief of staff, Marshall demurred. He told the president that whatever he decided, Marshall would "go along with it wholeheartedly. The issue was simply too great for any personal feeling to be involved."

In the end, Roosevelt told Marshall that he "could not sleep at night with you out of the country," and the assignment went to Dwight D. Eisenhower instead. Ike succeeded dramatically, became a national hero, and rode his fame all the way to the White House. Some people might interpret Marshall's actions as a sign of weakness, but nothing was further from the truth.

Indeed, in Marshall's case, his quiet and modest demeanor masked tremendous drive and a will of iron. Thankfully for the free world, his ambition and willpower were not personal or selfish in nature, but directed solely toward the purpose of serving his country by defeating our enemies. He was ruthless in his decision making when the issue of winning the war was at stake.

In his book *Good to Great*, noted business author Jim Collins describes corporate CEOs who embody this combination of extreme personal humility with great professional determination as Level 5 Leaders. Collins and his team studied companies that made a leap from good results to great results and sustained those levels of performance for at least fifteen years. These companies produced stock returns during those fifteen years that beat the general stock market by an average of seven times.

While Collins expressly sought to avoid a conclusion that these stellar results were due primarily to great leadership ("Ignore the executives," he told his research team), he could not overlook the overwhelming data that proved that in fact Level 5 leadership was key. Every single company on the roster had Level 5 leadership at the time they made the transition from good to great.

Collins observes, "Level 5 leaders are a study in duality: modest and willful, humble and fearless. To quickly grasp this concept, think of United States President Abraham Lincoln (one of few Level 5 presidents in United States history), who never let his ego get in the way of his primary ambition for the larger cause of an enduring great nation. Yet those who mistook Mr. Lincoln's personal modesty, shy nature, and awkward manner as signs of weakness found themselves terribly mistaken...."

Collins identifies such CEOs as Darwin Smith, who led Kimberly-Clark from 1971-1991, and Colman Mockler, CEO of Gillette from 1975 to 1991, as classic examples of Level 5 leaders who achieved extraordinary results during their tenures, but who were also always quick to give credit to others (not surprisingly, neither man is a household name today). Collins was "struck by how the good-to-great leaders *didn't* talk about themselves... It wasn't just false modesty. Those who worked with or wrote about the good-to-great leaders used words like *quiet, humble, modest, reserved, shy, gracious...* and so forth."

Finally, in contrast, Collins also found that in two-thirds of the companies against which he compared the good-to-great companies, leaders with enormous egos not only did not perform as well, but frequently "contributed to the demise or continued mediocrity of the company."

Where do you, your boss, and the rest of the leaders in your organization fall on the humility spectrum? Today, the simple truth is that we need more leaders like George Marshall, Darwin Smith, and Colman Mockler- people who show humility while striving to accomplish great things for the institutions they serve.

– PART FIVE–
LEARNING

"Learn from yesterday, live for today,
hope for tomorrow."

– Albert Einstein

– CHAPTER THIRTY-THREE –
ACTIVELY MANAGE
YOUR CAREER

"All the world's a stage,
And all the men and women merely players;
They have their exits and their entrances;
And one man in his time plays many
parts...."

– *As You Like It* 2.7, l.139-142

In a recent interview in the *New York Times*, Ford Motor Company President and CEO Alan Mulally was asked to provide his best career advice. He responded, "Don't manage your career. Think about just exceeding expectations in every job you do, continually ask for feedback on how you can do a better job, and the world will beat down your door to ask you to do more..."

I respectfully disagree with Mr. Mulally. While exceeding expectations and seeking feedback are important, I have found in my experience that success and advancement come most often to those individuals who actively manage their careers.

I spent more than a decade in human resources at Target and Best Buy. I can't count the number of times that people came to me frustrated over their perceived lack of career progress. The common theme sounded like this: "I work really hard. Feedback is positive.

Performance reviews are good. Yet no one seems to notice. The best opportunities go to others."

What I frequently found was that many of these individuals simply assumed that if they "exceeded expectations," someone would notice and ensure that their career moved forward. In addition, some of these folks could not answer the most fundamental question: What do I want to do with my career?

There may be lots of people — your supervisor, colleagues, human resource professionals, mentors — who think highly of you and will work to help you advance in your career. But, trust me, no one is going to do it for you. You must take personal responsibility for actively managing your own career.

And if you are going to manage your career, you need to know to what end. Ask yourself some tough questions, and be honest about the answers: Am I happy in my current job? Is it challenging and rewarding? Do I have room to grow, or have I hit a plateau? Where would I like to be one year, two years, or five years from now? Backing up from those goals, what affirmative steps must I take now to get there? In short, you need to be able to clearly answer the question: What do I want to do with my career?

Don't measure your progress or self-worth solely by money, title, power, or prestige. It is great to be ambitious, and we need people in corporate America (like Alan Mulally) who want to rise to the top of their organizations. But remember, just one person gets to be CEO. For the rest of us (at some point) we top out. If you are only seeking more money or the next title, you will be forever unhappy, because someone else will always be making more money or outrank you.

Consider other measures of success. Is your work interesting? Are your skills put to the test? Are you learning new things? Do you receive recognition for your efforts? Do you believe in the mission of your company? Are you adding not just to the bottom line for your organization, but creating value for society as a whole? Does your work match up with your personal values? Consider the definition of career success as broadly as you can, with a focus on those internal measures of satisfaction that are personally important to you.

I do agree with Alan Mulally on the criticality of feedback. In order to successfully manage your career, you need to be in a continuous cycle of seeking, receiving, absorbing, and adjusting to constant feedback. Seek feedback from as many different sources as possible, not just from your boss. Find those one or two really valuable people who will unfailingly give you honest feedback on how you are doing. Listen carefully to what they say. Insist on specifics.

If you are told you lack good communication skills, ask for details. Do you need to work on written skills? Spoken skills? Ask for examples of when you have fallen short and suggestions on how to improve.

Make changes based on the feedback you receive. Demonstrate flexibility and a willingness to learn and grow. Put together a personal development plan with clear milestones and share it with your boss and other trusted advisors. Work that plan with seriousness of purpose. Adjust the plan when appropriate as your career moves forward.

Finally, don't think of leadership or advancement in your career as simply a matter of managing a checklist, like a Boy or Girl Scout completing activities to earn a merit badge. Sometimes people would say to me, "I've done the three things you told me to do… now I'm ready to be promoted, right?" The very fact that they asked that question told me they weren't ready. Think of leadership and your career not in terms of finishing a to-do list, but as an ongoing journey- sometimes a complex and difficult journey.

Managing one's career is challenging, even in the best of times. These days, when so many of us are in crisis-mode, reacting to rather than shaping the reality around us, career management frequently goes to the back burner. Don't let it.

Remember these suggestions:

- Take responsibility for actively managing your own career.
- Develop a clear picture of what you want to do with your career.
- Measure success broadly, with a focus on intrinsic factors that are important to you.
- Seek specific, actionable feedback and respond appropriately.
- Put together a personal development plan and work it with energy.
- Consider leadership and career progress as a journey.

With these tips in mind, go forth and take advantage of your time on the stage, playing many roles during the course of a great career. Enjoy the adventure.

– CHAPTER THIRTY-FOUR –
SIMPLIFY AND PRIORITIZE

"Simplicity is an indispensable element of a leader's most important functions."

– Jack Welch

I know an executive who has a forty-page list of personal action items. Not forty items, total, on his to-do list, but forty pages, single-spaced, in a bound notebook. I have had professional dealings with this leader and I can tell you from first-hand experience that while he is a terribly busy man with a lot to do, he gets absolutely nothing done. He does not follow up on the most basic tasks, like returning phone calls or responding to e-mails. He cannot be counted on to deliver an outcome on anything. He tries to do everything, yet he accomplishes nothing. He is in a position of real power and his organization suffers greatly for his complete lack of focus. He has failed to adhere to that most fundamental yet important leadership principle: simplify and prioritize.

Simplifying and prioritizing starts with each of us as an individual leader. If we don't know what we are trying to accomplish in our own jobs, then there is no chance that the teams we lead will be any better focused.

In a recent interview the CEO of Continental Airlines, Lawrence

Kellner, was asked how he manages his time. He replied, "I used to have a long, long to-do list. At the end of the day, I'd see which ones got done. Then five more notes might be on my desk, and I'd throw them on the list. I realized I was often doing what came to me as opposed to what was really important. So I started saying, 'O.K., what are the three most important things I need to do today?' And if No. 1 is a twelve-hour task, then I'll spend the day working on it. I need to decide what's the most value-added thing I can do." In short, Kellner succeeded in taking charge of his professional life by proactively prioritizing his efforts, rather than simply reacting to whatever was in front of him. How well do you practice this skill as a leader?

Once we have our own priorities in order, the next task involves making sure our organizations and teams know what their priorities need to be. Again, Kellner is a model of good leadership in this regard. He says, "When I became CEO, I started ending each of my three most important meetings each month by saying, 'O.K., here are the three most important things we're doing. Here are the three priorities.'" His followers at Continental were no doubt grateful to him for explaining in clear and concrete terms exactly what he expected of them.

Great leaders instinctively understand that their teams are looking to them to identify just a small handful of key objectives, three or four at the most, and to communicate those objectives effectively. William Green is the chairman and chief executive of Accenture, the global consulting, technology services, and outsourcing company.

Green relates a story about how he was able to simplify things for a group of brand new employees: "I once sat through a three-day training session for new managers. I counted sixty-eight things we told them they needed to do to be successful. And I got up to close the session, and I said there are three things that matter. The first is competence... The second one is confidence... The third thing is caring..." He successfully narrowed the focus from sixty-eight things to three. This group of Accenture managers surely appreciated their chief's willingness to help them prioritize in their jobs and in their leadership journey.

Cristóbal Conde is the president and CEO of SunGuard, a software and IT services company, and he was notorious early in his career for micromanaging and making every decision himself. He soon realized the futility of this approach. He recalls, "That was in the early '90s, and that experience convinced me that the right way to do it is the opposite, which is to hold people accountable, to really restrict the number of things you say to them, and to decide the one or two things that are most important. You have to do that consistently over a year before you start having an impact." Indeed, it takes time to hammer a message home, but if it is simple and consistent, people will eventually respond and deliver.

Alan Mulally has been the president and chief executive of Ford Motor since 2006, and has led that company to extraordinary levels of achievement and value creation in an incredibly challenging time for the auto industry. Mulally is another leader who stays focused on a few key objectives. He says, "I've moved to a place where I'm really focused on four things. I pay attention to everything, but there are some things that are very unique to what I need to do as a leader. One of them is this process of connecting what we're doing to the outside world… A second focus for me is: What business are we in? What are we going to focus on? The third one is balancing the near term with the longer term… And then I really focus on values and standards… I'm the one who needs to focus on those four things, because if I do that, the entire team will have an understanding of them."

Albert Einstein once said, "Any intelligent fool can make things bigger, more complex, and more violent. It takes a touch of genius — and a lot of courage — to move in the opposite direction." The best leaders have an uncanny ability to simplify what is complex. They know what is truly important and what is not. They can identify the most critical challenges before them and prioritize those challenges so as to maximize their precious time. And they communicate these simple priorities to their team, again and again, in a way that helps people know how to direct their own efforts and to achieve results. Great leaders are incredibly adept at simplifying and prioritizing.

– CHAPTER THIRTY-FIVE –
BE PRESENT, LISTEN, AND LEARN

"The first duty of love is to listen."

– Paul Tillich

I love the game of golf. For the most part, I stink as a player, but I still enjoy golf. I'm not exactly sure what keeps me coming back for more, but I do know that I really appreciate the (only occasional) satisfaction of hitting a perfectly struck shot. When a golf shot is flawless the swing seems effortless, the ball jumps squarely off the clubface, and the trajectory, distance, and direction all mesh sublimely. It is a thing of beauty. I find that virtually the only time I succeed in delivering such a shot is when I am focused solely on the task at hand. I am neither worried about the putt I just missed on the last hole, nor what I will do on the upcoming par five. I am concerned only about the shot I am about to hit. I am right here, right now. In some cases, my mind even goes strangely blank. As a prelude to a perfect shot, sometimes I'm really not thinking about anything at all. I'm at peace with myself, in the present moment.

One would think that this keen awareness of the criticality of being in the present would enable a golfer to hit a perfect shot every time. But the reality is that "being present," in golf or any other endeavor, is an incredibly difficult thing to accomplish.

I believe that a lack of strong listening skills is a major impediment to productivity in the workplace, as well as to healthy outcomes in all other human interactions. I personally have never learned anything while I was doing the talking. Just as in golf, poor listeners are the ones who are either stewing about what was said five minutes ago, or anxiously anticipating their future response to what is being said right now. They are not in the present. They are not truly attentive. Conversely, the best listeners and most effective leaders are those who succeed in being present in the conversation, listening carefully, and learning as a result.

Dan Rosensweig is the president and chief executive of Chegg, a company that rents textbooks online and via mail. In a recent interview he was asked about how he runs meetings. He responded, "Probably the biggest lesson I've learned recently is to be present, because it's so easy to get distracted in the worlds of BlackBerrys, iPhones, Twitter, Facebook and 500 e-mails a day. So with our management team, when we're in a meeting, it starts on time, it ends on time, no technology. It's just, let's stay focused, and we have a much more healthy conversation. It works well in your personal life as well — wherever you are, be all in." But as Rosensweig strongly implies, with the manic pace of today's world, it is a terrific challenge to ever "be all in."

David Rome is a senior fellow at the Garrison Institute, a research and retreat center that applies contemplative methods to addressing social and environmental issues. He is a certified Focusing Trainer and a practicing Buddhist who, along with co-facilitator Hope Martin, teaches a seminar called Deep Listening.

In an article in the July 2010 issue of the periodical *Shambhala Sun*, Rome and Martin describe the tortured and angry nature of the recent debate on U.S. health care reform. They write, "The health care imbroglio may be an extreme example, but it reflects a larger pathology in our culture, one that is driven by adversarialness on the one hand and disingenuousness on the other. If we are to survive in the twenty-first century we must become better communicators, speaking and listening honestly and compassionately across diversity and difference.... A fruitful place to begin work on shifting our patterns of communication is with the quality of our *listening*. Just as we now understand the importance of exercise for good health, we need to exercise and strengthen our ability as listeners."

What steps can we take to become better listeners? Paradoxically, Rome and Martin suggest that effective Deep Listening begins with self-awareness. By paying better attention to ourselves we can better communicate with others. They write, "Deep Listening involves listening, from a deep, receptive, and caring place in oneself, to deeper and often subtler levels of meaning and intention in the other person. It is listening that is generous, empathic, supportive, accurate, and trusting. Trust here does not imply agreement, but the trust that whatever others say, regardless of how well or poorly it is said, comes from something true in their experience."

Rome and Martin suggest that "a clouded mirror cannot reflect accurately." In other words, unless and until we are true to ourselves, we cannot genuinely care about and compassionately listen to the concerns of others.

The next time you find yourself in the position of listener, consider your reactions to the situation. Are you able to separate your own selfish interests from those of the speaker? Do you immediately begin to think: How will this affect me? Are you frustrated with the person's speaking style or choice of words? Are you mentally jumping to your own response or even interrupting the speaker so that you can get your way more quickly? We are all guilty of these transgressions from time to time.

Instead of listening poorly, consider an attempt at Deep Listening. Be self-aware regarding your own impatience or disagreement and work to overcome it. Give yourself the opportunity and the time to really hear the other person. Provide your open-minded, fully focused attention. Attempt not just to comprehend on a superficial level, but to truly understand the other person's point of view as well as his/her needs, motives, and objectives. In short, be present and all in, right there at that very moment. You will be amazed at how much you will learn and how much progress the people in your organization will make. You will be more happy and satisfied in every other relationship in your life. And, though it may be a long shot, you may even improve in your golf game.

– CHAPTER THIRTY-SIX –
FOLLOW YOUR BLISS

"Far away there in the sunshine are my highest aspirations. I may not reach them, but I can look up and see their beauty, believe in them, and try to follow where they lead."

– Louisa May Alcott

I believe there is high honor in all work. Whether a person labors as a ditch digger, plumber, middle manager, homemaker, or chief justice of the U.S. Supreme Court, if that individual is willing to put in a full day of honest work, he or she deserves respect. I also strongly believe that people should take to heart the advice of the great mythologist, author, and teacher, Joseph Campbell, who instructed a generation of his students, "Follow your bliss."

A recent run of hilarious television beer commercials features the "Most Interesting Man in the World," who dispenses wisdom on a whole range of subjects in addition to malted beverages. In one spot he provides career advice, looking deeply into the camera and saying, "Find out what it is in life that you don't do well…. and then don't do that thing…. stay thirsty my friends." I take that same concept, but work to spin it into a positive when I tell my two daughters (who, like most teenagers, have myriad interests but have not yet settled on a specific path) to find out what they love to do in life, and then go do that thing.

In a unique and captivating book called, *Shop Class As Soulcraft: An Inquiry Into the Value of Work*, author Mathew B. Crawford contrasts the "symbolic knowledge work" that predominates in the corporate world of today with the age-old experience of making and fixing things with one's hands. Crawford has a Ph.D. in political philosophy from the University of Chicago and works as a fellow at the Institute for Advanced Studies in Culture at the University of Virginia. He also follows his bliss as a tinkerer with an intense interest in all things mechanical, and he owns a motorcycle repair shop in Richmond, Virginia.

In *Shop Class As Soulcraft*, Crawford seeks to restore the honor of the manual trades as a worthy pursuit, even in our high-tech, global economy. Crawford laments that "In the 1990s.... shop class started to become a thing of the past as educators prepared students to become 'knowledge workers.'" The problem with this effort to move people through high school and college and into the cubicle as knowledge workers is that it undervalues labor that involves the manipulation of things rather than ideas.

The typical office worker is overwhelmed with administrative details, budgets, planning meetings, and evaluations that often provide precious little sense of real progress or accomplishment. It is frequently difficult to measure one's individual impact in any tangible way. Crawford contrasts this with an electrician's precise knowledge that the job has been successfully completed when the light switch goes on, or the satisfaction of a skilled mechanic who gets a broken motorcycle to run again .

Crawford emphasizes that the manual trades are different from assembly line work and even many forms of white collar drudgery in that they require careful thinking. He says, "It may be that I am just not well-suited to office work. But in this respect I doubt there is anything unusual about me. I offer my own story here not because I think it is extraordinary, but rather because I suspect it is fairly common.... This book grows out of an attempt to understand the greater sense of agency and competence I have always felt doing manual work, compared with other jobs that are officially recognized as 'knowledge work.' Perhaps most surprisingly, I often find manual work more engaging intellectually."

Ultimately, although he does not expressly say it this way, Crawford passionately advocates that each individual must follow his or her bliss, whether as a knowledge worker, a manual laborer, or in some other way.

So many of us "just work for a living." We do our jobs as best we can, and we strive hard to support our families, but we get no particular energy nor do we take any special joy in doing what we do. We fail to follow our true bliss.

I was just such a person for better than twenty years, laboring as an office/cube-dwelling knowledge worker. I was fortunate to be employed by some great organizations, liked my co-workers, and enjoyed certain aspects of my responsibilities. I was thankful to be employed and understood full well how lucky I was — particularly in a tough economy — to have a steady paycheck. But at the end of day, as is true for so many people, mine was "just a job."

In early 2009 I struck off on my own as an entrepreneur, working to build a company that provides leadership training, workshops, and consulting services. I also took time to write a book and a regular business column. Goodness knows I am no mechanic, and I still spend lots of time sitting at a desk looking at a computer screen; nevertheless, with as much certainty as at any point in my life, I am following my bliss. Despite the occasional "entrepreneurial anxiety attack," I am also the happiest I have ever been in my work life. I feel richly blessed for the opportunity and encourage everyone, in whatever form it may take, to follow his or her bliss.

In his book, *The Power of Myth*, Joseph Campbell summarizes, "I always tell my students, go where your body and soul want to go. When you have that feeling, then stay with it, and don't let anyone throw you off." He goes on to say, "I even have a superstition that…. if you do follow your bliss you put yourself on a kind of track that has been there all the while, waiting for you, and the life you ought to be living is the one you are living…. I say follow your bliss and don't be afraid, and doors will open where you didn't know they were going to be."

– CHAPTER THIRTY-SEVEN –
WORK DIFFERENTLY

"Even though worker capacity and motivation are destroyed when leaders choose power over productivity, it appears that bosses would rather be in control than have the organization work well."

– Margaret Wheatley

As an entrepreneur and writer who has worked out of a home office for the past eighteen months, I have been spared the aggravation of sitting in traffic, something which used to bother me a lot when commuting to and from a corporate location. Some days my travel time was up to two hours long. Recently, I had to drive to meet a colleague who could only do so first thing in the morning and, guess what, I got stuck in traffic. As I sat there stewing over the annoying waste of my time, I also looked around me and considered what an unproductive and stressful situation a traffic jam represents for everyone involved. I was thankful for the opportunity I've had in recent times as an individual business owner to work differently and frankly, much more fruitfully. I was also reminded with renewed appreciation of the reality that successful companies are now coming around to the idea of allowing their employees to work differently too, with a focus on productive outcomes rather than long hours spent with butts in chairs.

American workers are growing increasingly disenchanted with their jobs, in a way that presents a potentially serious problem as we all strive to compete in a global economy. While most working Americans might say they feel fortunate just to have a job given the current unemployment rate, a 2009 survey of 5,000 households by the Conference Board revealed that only 45 percent of Americans are satisfied with their work, which represents the worst result in that category in twenty-two years of surveys. The recession undoubtedly accounts for some of the unhappiness, but job satisfaction has been in decline for more than twenty years.

The Conference Board highlighted additional troubling numbers: only 51 percent of Americans find their work interesting; 64 percent of workers under age twenty-five are unhappy in their jobs; only 43 percent of workers feel secure in their jobs; just 51 percent are satisfied with their boss; and a mere 56 percent are satisfied with their commute to work. Among other issues, weak wage growth and increased health care costs have been concerns over the past two decades. But the drudgery entailed in so many jobs in our modern economy of traveling to and from an office to sit in a cube and stare at a computer screen all day must be a factor as well. One of the study's authors, Lynn Franco, says, "What's really disturbing about growing job dissatisfaction is the way it can play into the competitive nature of the U.S. workforce down the road and on the growth of the U.S. economy, all in a negative way."

Good companies are attempting to address this malady. In a fascinating — albeit painful — experiment in which I personally participated during my years at Best Buy, two courageous innovators named Jody Thompson and Cali Ressler endeavored to introduce the company to a concept they called the "Results-Only Work Environment," or ROWE. The ROWE concept emphasizes a change in focus from hours to outcomes, and allows employees to control when, where, and how long they work, as long as they meet their business objectives.

Jody and Cali faced significant resistance in some corners of the company, mostly because Best Buy proudly nurtured a culture of long hours and hard work in both the store and headquarters environments. Managers feared abuse of the system and doubted that better outcomes might be achieved. I remember one skeptical manager telling an employee who was out of the office that, "You need to ROWE, ROWE, ROWE your ass back to work."

Nevertheless, over time, business results spoke for themselves. Departments at Best Buy that implemented ROWE saw productivity increases that averaged 35 percent, as well as sharp decreases in voluntary turnover rates of as much as 90 percent in some business units. Jody and Cali have now left Best Buy and taken their show on the road via their company, CultureRx, to encourage other organizations to adopt the power of ROWE.

To be sure, some jobs simply cannot be accomplished other than in a specific work location, such as a retail store or manufacturing facility. Many people would be loath to work in a virtual environment because they enjoy the daily personal interaction with their co-workers. Some folks would be distracted at home and need the discipline of an office environment to stay on task.

But the trend toward more flexible hours and working from home is undeniable, and the potential impact of developing a more virtual economy is huge. Last year, according to market research firm Interactive Data Corp., 18.4 million Americans (like me) worked in homebased businesses, and the expectation is for that number to increase by 350,000 per year for the next several years. Further, a study by the Telework Research Network estimates that if everyone who could work from home — approximately 40 percent of the workforce — did so just half the time, the annual impact would be staggering:

- American companies would realize $200 billion in productivity gains.
- Companies would save $190 billion on such things as reduced real estate expenses, electricity bills, absenteeism, and turnover.
- Greenhouse gas emissions would be reduced by 50 million tons, and 276 million barrels of oil (32 percent of imports from the Middle East) would be saved.
- American business would save a total of $700 billion.

How flexible is your company or organization around work schedules? Does your team feel that they enjoy good work-life balance? Do you as a leader of people focus on the number of hours worked or on good business outcomes? If what matters most in your organization is the perception of grinding out long hours in a traditional office setting, maybe it's time to try a more flexible approach. Your business will be the better for your effort to think and work differently.

– CHAPTER THIRTY-EIGHT –
SUCCEED IN LEARNING FROM FAILURE

"Sweet are the uses of adversity;
Which, like the toad, ugly and venomous,
Wears yet a precious jewel in his head..."

– *As You Like It* 2.1, l.12-14

In the early 1920s a young artist and animator who lived in Kansas City set out to form his own company, which would specialize in producing cartoons. He hired his first employee and secured a deal with a local theater owner to air the cartoons, which were called "Newman Laugh-O-Grams." The cartoons became popular in the local area, and soon the budding entrepreneur signed a stable of animators to help his studio, also called Laugh-O-Gram, to increase production. Unfortunately, the tiny enterprise became top-heavy with salaries and began to lose money. The fledgling tycoon had to shut down the business and declare bankruptcy. This man went on to become one of the most successful and revered business leaders in American history, but he never forgot the pain of his initial setback, or what he learned. In later years, as he looked back on the experience, he said, "It is important to have one good hard failure when you are young." His name was Walt Disney.

When I was a young man in my early thirties, I quit the practice of law to go into business for myself. I formed an S Corporation, opened a fast-food franchise, and had to rapidly educate myself as to the ins and outs of Small Business 101. It was an amazing learning experience for me and (long hours aside) I loved the freedom of being my own boss.

Despite my best efforts, however, I could not generate sufficient revenue to cover my costs. I stayed in business for about six months and then, reluctantly, was forced to close up shop. I had a wife and small child who depended on me. I had lost all our savings and was bankrupt. I was unemployed for seven months. There was no sugarcoating it: I had failed miserably, in a way that had never happened to me before. Nevertheless, this incredibly difficult passage from almost twenty years ago shaped who I am in ways that still resonate to this day. In its way, it was a much more significant and life-changing event for me than any of my triumphs have ever been. Painful though it was, like Walt Disney, I succeeded in learning from failure.

University of Virginia psychology professor Jonathan Haidt writes in his book *The Happiness Hypothesis*, "People need adversity, setbacks and perhaps even trauma to reach the highest levels of strength and fulfillment. Suffering is not always all bad for all people. There is usually some good mixed in with the bad, and those who find it have found something precious: a key to moral and spiritual development."

In his book *The Pursuit of Perfect*, Harvard professor Tal Ben-Shahar argues that individuals who risk failure actually tend to be happier than those who are averse to challenge and change. Ben-Shahar says, "Successful people are necessarily people who have failed many times, and therefore are 'better' at failing than others. When we practice failure, we realize the pain associated with fear of failure is often greater than the pain associated with actual failures."

The roster of well-known people who have achieved at a high level in their lives but who have also learned from failure along the way is endless. Former President Bill Clinton says, "When I was defeated for reelection as governor in 1980, there didn't seem to be much future for me in politics. I was probably the youngest ex-governor in American history. But if I hadn't been defeated, I probably never would have become president. It was a near-death experience, but it forced me to be more sensitive and to understand that if people think you've stopped listening, you're sunk."

Author J.K. Rowling, who penned the mega-best-selling *Harry Potter* series of books, was at one time alone, unemployed, and "as poor as it is possible to be in modern Britain without being homeless." But for Rowling, "Failure meant a stripping away of the inessential. I stopped pretending to myself that I was anything other than what I was, and began directing all of my energy into finishing the only work that mattered to me."

Indeed, these days, many companies actually look to actively recruit workers who have experienced and overcome adversity in their personal or professional lives. Meridee Moore is the founder of Watershed Asset Management, a $2 billion hedge fund in San Francisco. When asked in a recent interview about how she hires, Moore responded, "… if the person has had a rough patch in the past, that's usually good... if you've ever had a setback and come back from it, I think it helps you make better decisions. There's nothing better for sharpening your ability to predict outcomes than living through some period where things went wrong. You've learned that no matter how smart you are and how hard you work, you have to anticipate things that can go against you."

The Great Recession has been a huge challenge for all of us. Many of us have experienced defeats and even real suffering, both in our jobs and on the home front. But there can be redemption. The phoenix can rise again from the ashes. For me, out of my spectacular failure, I learned many things. I learned to take new challenges seriously, and never to assume that skills and abilities that have pulled me through in the past will necessarily pull me through the next time. I learned to worry only about those things that I can control, and the main thing I control on a daily basis is my attitude. I get to choose how I want to be. I learned to appreciate my many blessings, especially good health, family, and friends. And I learned a whole lot about humility.

Professor Ben-Shahar of Harvard summarizes the idea well: "The ones who will emerge stronger from [adversity] — the resilient ones — are those who learn to find the opportunity in every setback." In short, they are the people who succeed in learning from failure.

– CHAPTER THIRTY-NINE –
RECHARGE YOUR BATTERIES

"If I were a medical man, I should prescribe a holiday to any patient who considered his work important."

– Edward O. Wilson

Summer is almost over. I just returned from a wonderful long weekend with family and friends on a placid little lake in northwestern Connecticut. I came home happy, rested, and ready to go back to work. I am reminded once again of the importance of taking time to recharge one's batteries.

Recently, President Obama and his family spent time at Martha's Vineyard, that scenic and idyllic spot off the southern coast of Cape Cod. When word of the First Family's vacation plans first came out, controversy erupted. How could the chief executive be taking time off when there are so many pressing issues at hand? We need him on duty. America is fighting two wars. The economy is in recession. Workers are unemployed. We are facing crises with the environment and health care. There is so much to do.

I understand how people feel, but (politics aside) can't we all agree that our commander-in-chief needs to be healthy, energized, and clear-thinking in everything that he does?

Certainly, there is a lot on all of our plates. For many families facing tough economic times, a vacation is not possible right now based on personal finances. But recharging one's batteries is not achieved solely by taking time off in some remote, exotic location. We can refuel the tank every day, in simple ways, by just learning to relax and divert our attention from time to time.

In a recent interview in *Harvard Business Review*, Pulitzer-Prize-winning historian Doris Kearns Goodwin, who has written several presidential biographies, was asked about the essential qualities of a great leader. She listed a few and then said, "I would add here that one more success factor is key for great leadership, be it in business or politics, and it's one that's usually overlooked. As a leader you need to know how to relax so that you can replenish your energies for the struggles facing you tomorrow."

Dr. Goodwin went on to say, "Lincoln went to the theater about a hundred times while he was in Washington. And although he suffered from a certain melancholy, he had a tremendous sense of humor and would entertain people long into the night with his stories. Franklin Roosevelt was the same way. He had this cocktail hour every evening during World War II when you just couldn't talk about the war. He needed to remain free from thinking about the bad things for a few hours. Or he would play with his stamps. This ability to recharge your batteries in the midst of great stress and crisis is crucial for successful leadership."

There are many other historical examples. John Kennedy loved to paint, sail, and play golf. Winston Churchill loved to paint, write books, smoke cigars, and drink scotch whiskey. Harry Truman loved to take a brisk walk every day, play poker, and drink bourbon whiskey. (Anecdotal evidence aside, there is no solid data that proves that drinking whiskey results in success as a leader.) The current occupant of the White House is also a poker player, and enjoys golf and basketball.

There is an additional challenge these days in that we are all so intensely, immediately connected and networked that many of us feel we simply can't take time off or the earth will stop spinning without us. Or perhaps we are secretly worried that if we take time to relax, we will realize the harsh reality that business, and life, will indeed go on without us. We don't want to find out the awful truth that we are not individually essential to world progress.

Dr. Goodwin offers a fascinating perspective on this phenomenon. She comments on how in the nineteenth century, busy as leaders were, they took time to pen lengthy letters. She says, "Looking back, the thing that's really impressive is that here were these leaders running the Civil War, and people like [Secretary of State William] Seward still had time to meditate on the day's events and to write these long letters to his wife at night. These were the days of no television. Leaders weren't worried about cable news or their BlackBerrys. They weren't multitasking; they had time to reflect. It's a luxury many leaders just don't have today, and that's a real loss."

When was the last time you truly paused to take a breath and contemplate life? That you read a fun book just to escape? That you exercised or got outside for some fresh air and sunshine? That you noticed nature's awesome beauty? That you enjoyed quality time with your family or friends? That you actually wrote a letter out in longhand and sent it to someone via snail mail? That you pursued a hobby that enables you to become so focused on what you are doing that you are just in the moment for a little while, unaware of the trials and tribulations of the world around you?

If the answer is "not recently," then please take a serious look at what you need to do to arrange your life so that these things can happen for you from time to time. You will be a better person for it and, as a result of that, also a better leader.

In the end, we all occasionally need to take the advice of that famous and wise philosopher, Tommy Bahama, who reminds us to just "Relax…."

– CHAPTER FORTY –
FORGE AHEAD FOR TIME IS PRECIOUS

"You're only dancing on this earth
for a short while."

– From the song "Oh Very Young," by Cat Stevens

I love the discipline and the process of writing. I toil away on a
desktop computer in my study at home. On the wall to my left as I
work at my desk, just next to my bookshelves, hangs a photographic
portrait of General (and later President) Ulysses S. Grant. The photo
was taken in 1864 near Cold Harbor, Virginia, during the darkest
days of the American Civil War. Grant wears the rumpled, plain-blue
garb of a three-star Union general (he commanded all of the Northern armies at the time), and he takes a relaxed pose while standing
on muddy ground outside of his headquarters tent, one hand resting
against a tree and the other on his hip. The fighting at Cold Harbor
was some of the most terrible of the entire war. One can almost see
a hint of pain and sadness in Grant's bearded, care-worn face as he
looks unsmiling at the camera. But his visage, reflective of the overwhelming responsibility of his position and the awful life-and-death
decisions he was required to make, also projects high intelligence,
quiet confidence, extreme focus, and grim determination.

The portrait is situated such that Grant looks directly at me — his gaze is intense — while I write. When my attention wanders or my energy wanes, this picture serves as an inspirational reminder that I must forge ahead, for time is precious.

Grant was born in 1822 in Ohio and was a middling student at West Point. He fought bravely in every significant engagement of the Mexican War in the 1840s. After the war he developed an unfortunate fondness for alcohol, left the army, and experienced embarrassing failures as a businessman and farmer. As the contentious issues of slavery and secession came to a boil and war clouds gathered anew, Grant labored as a humble clerk in his father's dry goods store in Galena, Illinois.

With the onset of the Civil War in 1861, Grant returned to his one true calling and the profession at which he came to excel, arguably, beyond any other soldier in American history. He began the war as a regimental commander but was rapidly promoted, ultimately rising to the rank of lieutenant general and appointment by President Abraham Lincoln as general in chief of all U.S. forces. Grant proved a brilliant strategist and a stubborn fighter who won the war by ruthlessly using the superior numbers and material resources of his mighty armies to slowly but relentlessly bludgeon his formidable Southern enemy into submission.

Grant emerged as the great hero of the war and went on to serve two terms as the eighteenth president of the United States. Though he was himself a man of high personal integrity, Grant's administration was riddled with corruption, and his presidency is regarded by most historians as a failure.

In the 1880s, as a result of another unlucky business venture, Grant lost his entire life savings and fell heavily into debt. Friends had encouraged him to write his memoirs, but he was reluctant because he believed that there would be little interest in his story. Finally, for the purpose of taking care of his family he felt compelled to begin writing. The famous novelist and Grant's good friend Mark Twain volunteered to help him in the publication process. The effort to complete his *Personal Memoirs* became a profound struggle because in the same month he began to write (September 1884), Grant, who was a life-long cigar smoker, was diagnosed with inoperable throat cancer.

Grant now knew that time was truly precious because he was dying. He desired nothing more than to ensure that the person he loved above all others, his wife of thirty-six years, Julia Dent Grant, and their children, would be financially secure when he was gone. He threw himself into his mission with the same powerful determination that won the Civil War, writing mostly in pencil on a pad of paper, fighting incapacitating pain every hour of every day.

Historian Geoffrey Perret writes in his excellent biography, *Ulysses S. Grant: Soldier and President,* "Part of the secret of his success as a general stood revealed as he bent to his final task, not only in the power of his will but in the clarity of his mind. Drugs did not seem to color his thinking, nor did physical exhaustion, lack of sleep, intense pain, or impending oblivion. He treated all of these as irrelevant or, at most, irritants, and focused tightly on the task at hand." Grant finished the book on July 19, 1885, and three days later he was dead.

The opening words to the preface of *Personal Memoirs of U.S. Grant* contain a quotation borrowed from a fifteenth-century devotional book, and then Grant's understandably fatalistic observation concerning that quotation: " 'Man proposes and God disposes.' There are but few important events in the affairs of men brought about by their own choice."

The *Personal Memoirs* became a smashing success and to this day is regarded as a classic of American letters. Grant's dying wish came true as his family experienced a financial windfall from sales of the book. Sometimes, even sad stories can have a bittersweet, if not entirely happy ending.

Recently, a number of people in my wider network have either been diagnosed with or died from inoperable cancer. The wife of a former co-worker. The daughter of a close associate. The mother of a dear friend. A respected colleague, father, and friend with whom I worked years ago. Wonderful human beings all. I am continually reminded that life is fragile and fleeting. The flame burns brightly, but all too briefly, and then it goes out.

Wherever you may find yourself in your own journey, if you have a burden to overcome — take it on. If you have a task to complete — get going. If you have someone who needs to know that you love them — tell them. But through it all, don't forget to enjoy the here and the now. Take heed of the beautiful sentiment and powerful truth that is captured in the well-known quotation, "The past is history, the future is a mystery, but today is a gift; that's why they call it the present."

ACKNOWLEDGMENTS

"I can no other answer makes
but thanks, and thanks...."

– *Twelfth Night*, 3.3, l.15-16

My family is the most important thing in my life. To my beloved wife, Faith, and amazing daughters Anna and Lucia, to whom I dedicate this book, I will love you always. To my father, Carl; mother, Doris, and siblings Tom and Joan, thank you for your love and support over an entire lifetime. To my extended family, you all are great.

To Larry Werner for giving me a chance, sight unseen, to show you what I could do.

To my editor Anne Hodgson, for your perceptive intelligence; the book is much better for your efforts. To Emily Yost, for your design of the book jacket and interior and your special genius — you see things I could never see, and create outcomes I could never imagine. To my proofreader Sherri Hildebrandt for your good and careful work. To Jeannie Androsoff, for your help, loyal friendship, and concerted effort on behalf of my dream. It has been fun for the two of us to dream together. I can never thank you enough. To the many good people who helped produce the book at Beaver's Pond Press, and especially my good friend Dara Beevas.

To my Blue Knight board of advisors, who are the wise women and men who have kept the enterprise going: Ann Aronson, Gail Dorn, Jenney Egertson, Bill Gjetson, Mat Gjetson, Ellen Hinrichs,

Jeff Johnson, Traci Petschl, Randy Ross, Brent Siegel, and Jack Uldrich.

To the wonderful friends who make life worth living: Danal and Wendy Abrams, Jack El-Hai, Brian and Cathy Gauger, Al and Jill Hatfield, John Magnusson, Matt Moran, Charlie Newman, Val Johnson, Pete and Nancy Ross, Paul and Kathy Vaaler, and John and Jennifer Youngblood.

You are all, each one of you, terrific, and the book would not have been possible without your collective support and encouragement. I thank you from the bottom of my heart.